The Church of St Levan
❧ *A Guide & History* ❧

Susan Hoyle

The Hypatia Trust
Trevelyan House
Penzance, Cornwall
2007

For my father

This edition of *The Church of St Levan: A Guide & History* is published in 2007 by

Hypatia Publications
16 Chapel Street
Penzance, Cornwall TR18 4AW

© Susan Hoyle 2007 (text)
© Photographs held by individual photographers:
Lynn Batten, Susan Hoyle,
Andrew Hallam, Charles Roff

The right of Susan Hoyle to be identified as the Author of this Work has been asserted by her in accordance with the Copyright, Designs and Patents Act 1988.

All rights reserved.
No part of this publication may be reproduced or transmitted in any form or by any means without permission from the publishers.

ISBN 978-1-872229-55-3

Book design by Donna J. Anton

Printed in the United Kingdom
by Headland Press
Penzance, Cornwall

Table of Contents

List of Illustrations iv
Foreword v
How to use this book vii
Introduction ix

PART ONE – The Guide
Inside the Church of St Levan 1
General Description 1
The Tour 2
Outside the Church 25

PART TWO – The History
Christianity comes to West Penwith 31
The beginnings of St Levan Church 38
The Anglo-Saxon and Norman Church 41
A dependent chapel 44
The end of the Deanery and the creation of the Rectorship 84
The Modern Parish(es) 89

Appendix A: List of Clergy 99
Appendix B: Details of More Recent Incumbents 106
Appendix C: Discovering Church History 110
Appendix D: The Terrier 113
Notes 114
Bibliography 119
Acknowledgements 129

List of Illustrations

1. St Levan church, frontispiece *(Charles Roff)*
2. Transparency of woodcut of the Font (Sept. 17, 1849; artist unknown), title page
3. Woodcut of St Levan church by JT Blight (1876), p. vi
4. St Levan church, p. viii *(Lynn Batten)*
5. Sketch plan of St Levan church as it is today, p. x
6. Historical plan of the church, p. 3
7. The Font, p. 4 *(CR)*
8. Church interior, p. 5 *(CR)*
9. The South Porch, p. 7 *(CR)*
10. The Dairy, p. 8 *(LB)*
11. Roodscreen images, p. 12 *(LB)*
12. Christogram and instruments, p. 15 *(Susan Hoyle)*
13. Altar frontal, p. 17 *(SH)*
14. Rowena Cade altar frontal, p. 18 *(SH)*
15. Pew-ends Nos 17, 11, 14, 8, 7, 26, 13, pp. 21-24 *(Andrew Hallam, LB, SH)*
16. Sundial, Churchyard Cross *(AH)*; Cross with inscription *(CR)*, p. 27
17. The Stone and the church, p. 28 *(CR)*
18. Holy Well, p. 29 *(top photo LB; lower photo CR)*
19. St Levan church with lichened cross, p. 30 *(CR)*
20. Tracing of Selevan's name, p. 32 *(SH)*
21. The Stone, p. 36 *(AH)*
22. Woodcut of St Levan's Well by JT Blight, p. 38
23. Raftra wall, p. 39 *(SH)*
24. Deanery tithe list (ca 1450), p. 46 *(King's College Library, Cambridge)*
25. Image of William Polkinghorne's handwriting, p. 67 *(Cornwall Record Office) (SH)*
26. Image of John Clode's excuse to the Court, p. 73 *(Cornwall Record Office) (SH)*
27. The Deanery Seals, p. 74 *(Cornwall Record Office) (SH)*
28. James Bevan plaque, p. 77 *(CR)*
29. Roodscreen and Hodge stained-glass window, p. 83 *(LB)*
30. Newspaper photo of St Levan rectory after 1932 fire, p. 95
31. Woodcut of St Levan churchyard (ca 1849; artist unknown), p. 97
32. Evelyn Trimer Bennett pew inscription, p. 128 *(SH)*

Foreword

Histories of parish churches come in all shapes and sizes. Sometimes they simply describe a church and draw attention to special features in it. Others are much more detailed and use the jargon of ecclesiastical architecture that makes casual visitors wish they had a dictionary in their pocket.

Few, though, do what Susan Hoyle has done, in this history of St Levan Church, which replaces the booklet written by Jeffery Burr, who died just a few years ago.

First of all, we are taken into the church and given a very full and interesting description of the church building itself and its history and development and also an easily understood description of individual items within it – like, for instance, the font and, of course, the wonderful pew-ends, which are one of the church's particular glories.

The writer helps visitors and pilgrims understand and appreciate that the church building is itself a continuing story – and that the building is not a museum, but is still the House of God and the Gate of Heaven for parishioners and visitors alike.

Having introduced the church in this way, Susan Hoyle then puts the building in its historical and geographical context and helps the visitor to understand something about the very particular and dramatic nature of the building and its setting. For instance, we are given information about St Levan himself and the settlement that bears his name. We are told about the various legends that surround St Levan and the place, but we are also helped to see how the church and community were affected by national, political and ecclesiastical events such as the Reformation in the 16th century. Particularly dramatic is the story in this book of the relationship of Bishop Grandisson of Exeter with the parish and the events leading up to his visit there in 1336, with knights to guard him.

The history of the parish continues up to the present day, and the writer has consulted contemporary experts, as is clear in various references. This book, then, is a model, both for the visitor, and if I may say so, for a busy Diocesan Bishop who has to preach at occasions such as a dedication festival and needs to borrow local knowledge and appear to be well read!

So, please read this book, enjoy it and profit from it. It is a model of its kind and you would benefit from a close reading as well as using it just to look around the church.

The Rt Revd W. Ind
Bishop of Truro

How to use this book

There are two main parts to this book: the Guide and the History.

The first is a tour of St Levan Church, inside and out. These are pages to consult as you look around this lovely site, helping you to understand what you see and perhaps pointing out things you might otherwise miss. Following that is a brief account of the other monuments in the neighbourhood which 'belong' to the church: St Levan's Chapel and Well, the Crosses, and the Stone. They are all worth a visit.

The history is perhaps to read more at your leisure. It covers the coming of Christianity to the Land's End peninsula and to what is now St Levan, the stories of the saint, the development of the building and the parish, and something of what is known of the clergy.

Finally there is a list of sources of further information – books, websites and documents that will deepen your knowledge and appreciation of this and other churches, as they have mine.

This little volume replaces the very popular *History of the Church of St Levan*, written in 1994 by the late Jeffery C Burr. It brings that work up to date by taking account of recent scholarship and archæological discoveries, and by using the Internet to unearth hitherto neglected material.

INTRODUCTION

In the 1920s, Canon Doble, the great collector and teller of Cornish saints' lives, remarked that there were only two of 'his' saints whose stories survived in the contemporary mind and imagination: one was St Neot, and the other was St Levan (or Selevan, to give him his real name). He thought it significant that they were both fishermen, and that they both had holy wells associated with them.

St Levan Church here in the far west of Cornwall – almost at Land's End – has always been off the beaten track, remote and isolated. There was never a village around the church; the Churchtown has always been no more than a few houses. Indeed, until the Rectory was built a little over a century ago, even the clergy did not live nearby – and now that St Levan is part of a parish group again, the priest-in-charge once more lives away.

This inaccessibility was deliberate. It was an expression of an important aspect of Celtic Christianity, the belief that it is in seclusion that people come nearer to God. The first missionary at this place, the man whom we remember as St Levan, chose his spot carefully – his chapel is only a few hundred metres from here, down towards the beach now known as Porth Chapel – and for some 1,500 years, his choice has held.

And even he may not have lived here. Some say his house was at Bodellan, which, if you came via Porthcurno, you will have passed, and probably not noticed. Every day, we are told, he walked from there to his fishing-place over at Porth Chapel, along a path which is very likely the path that runs from Bodellan today, passing through the churchyard and down to the old chapel.

More of that in the History section of this little book. For now, we will explore the church, starting inside.

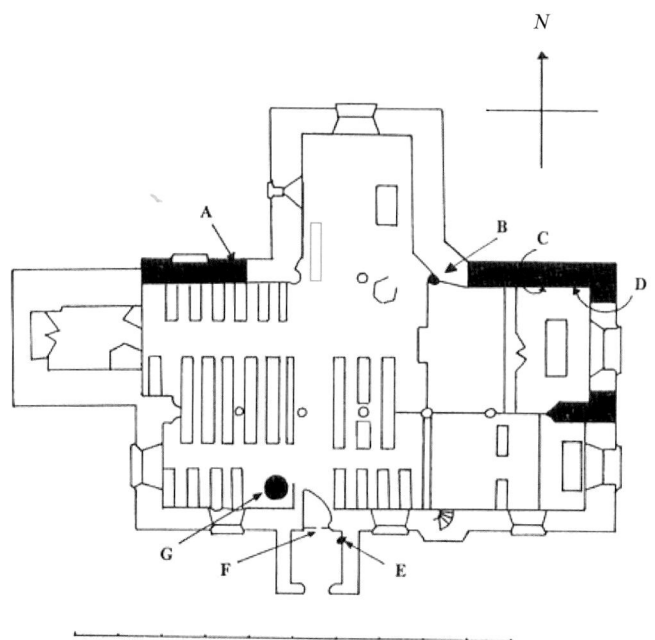

Sketch Plan of St Levan Church as it is today
showing the Norman survivals and approximate positions of church furniture
A – blocked north door; B – reused capital; C&D – newly exposed niches;
E – stoup; F – Norman arch; G – Norman font
Based on the plan in Jeffery Burr, *A History of the Church of St Levan* (amended 1997).
A more detailed map is on page 3.

❧ I ⚘

✠ ✠ ✠ ✠ ✠

Part One

INSIDE THE CHURCH OF ST LEVAN

Standing with one's back to the south door (where you came in): straight ahead is north, to your left is west and to your right, east. You probably already knew that, but the points of the compass are important in a church: here, as in most English and Cornish churches, the south door is, and has long been, the door through which the congregation arrives; the (now blocked) north door has a fascinating history of its own, as we shall see; at the west end is the tower (the most common place for it), and there was once an important door there too (blocked quite recently); and at the east end of the church is the chancel, historically the preserve of the clergy and the holiest part of the building, divided from the nave by what remains of the mediæval rood screen.

General Description

What you see today is much more what the Victorian architect-restorer wanted you to see than what a parishioner in, say, 1400 or 1500 would have seen; but we must be grateful that this building survived at all. It nearly did not. In the 1860s, there was a serious proposal to build a new church up in Polgigga, along the lane to Porthgwarra. This place would have been abandoned.

But it was not. Most guidebooks will tell you that the bulk of it is a late-14th-/early 15th-century rebuild, after the Black Death. However, work by Joanna Mattingly has established that it is a century younger than that – and the same goes for many other Cornish churches. The south aisle (immediately inside the door) was built soon after 1500, and work had already begun on a similar aisle on the north when the Reformation, with its quite different liturgical and financial demands, forced the parish and its churchwardens to stop.

The plan on page 3 is a rough guide to what was built, what was demolished, and what was planned, but never built. Apart from the stoup (sandstone) and some window cills, the stone is all granite.

The Norman church was constructed in the early 12th century (say, 1120-50), and was much smaller than the present one: it was cruciform, with a north transept smaller than the existing one. The south transept lay from about where the steps are now in the Lady Chapel to about the west end of the porch. Small parts of this Norman structure remain — especially on the north wall of both the chancel and the nave, and also in the arch above the south door. The existing north transept replaced the Norman one well before the Tudor rebuild, perhaps when the tower was built.

There was at least one even earlier church on this site: traces of an Anglo-Saxon building were found in 1997 when repair work was done to the internal walls. It was not big: its outline is within the walls of the existing chancel, and its size compares with St Levan's chapel, out on the cliff.

The Tour

The Porch

The present porch was built after the south aisle was completed, or so one assumes given the bad fit of the timbers with the statue-niche above the door. (The niche was for an image of St Levan.) The porch may have been added when work began on the north aisle. Porches were not just for sheltering from the weather. From Anglo-Saxon times, if not earlier, they were used for marriages. It was only after the couple were married that they crossed the threshold into the church, and their union was blessed. This custom changed after the Reformation, as church and state tried to control marriage more closely, but this did not mean that the porch was redundant. The benches may have been used for meetings; church-porches were traditional places for legal documents to be signed, for example.

The stoup on the right as you enter is Norman, a very good example of its type, and will originally have been placed to the side of the old entrance. The early 16th-century wagon roof is complete and original.

Historical Plan of the Church
Not to scale.

The church is aligned West (left) to East (right).

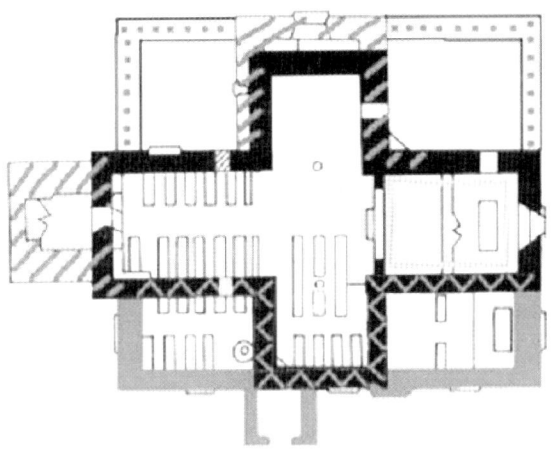

- Approx disposition of Anglo-Saxon church
- The Norman church c 1120
- 13th/14th-century additions
- Demolished 1520-40?
- Built 1520-40?
- Planned 1520-40? but never built
- Approx disposition of church furniture in 2006
- Suggested position of Norman south door
- Position of Norman north door

The Font and the south-west corner

To the left of the south door – the door you entered by – is the very handsome **font**. The font is often the oldest item in a church, and so it is here. This one is Norman, and is almost certainly from the church which stood here before this. Although some say that the Normans did not have tools to carve granite, this seems to be in a fine light granite.

On the wall in the south-west corner there are several **memorials** of interest to historians of this church. (Some of them were formerly in the chancel.) Reading from the left: the first is to the memory of the fourth Rector of St Levan, Trimer Bennett, who served here for 26 years from 1898. (St Levan had a rector only from 1864.) Above that is a plaque from 1880 to commemorate three men who worked for the Eastern Telegraph Company at Porthcurno, and beyond that another in memory of a choir-member who was also at the ETC. The station was also a training college for telegraphy: young men came here from all over the world and left to serve all over the world. The other plaque represents one of the chief families of St Levan over hundreds of years: the Hodge family. You will see many other memorials to them here.

The Font is Norman. The large bowl has a lower border of cable work, suggestive of a ship's rope anchoring the baptised soul to God, while the upper border is of carved crosses. Between, the decoration is of four identical patterns of stars and circles, meaning perhaps the heavens.

The **ceiling** in the south aisle is a restored 16th-century wagon roof, and you can see traces of paint still on the wood. The ceiling elsewhere is 19th-century.

The Tower and Bells

Moving across now to the **tower arch**, you can see here that the tower (two-staged and unbuttressed) was built separately from the body of the church. As is often the case, the tower is of a different date from the rest of the

Interior of the church, looking towards the chancel
and showing what an intimate church St Levan is.

The "Dairy" is on the left, and some of the roodscreen panels are
visible to the right of the pulpit. In late mediaeval times, the roodscreen
would have reached to the height of the pillar capitals, and above that a
large cross (or rood) would have been suspended.

building. This is because most parishes could not afford to pay for the whole building in one go, and so the tower appeared either a while before or a while after the main body of the church.

A church-tower points to the heavens, and also makes a statement about the parish: that it is rich enough, or devout enough, to provide for it. Its main purpose, however, is to house the bells, and this explains why the materials and construction of most church-towers are superior to the rest of the building. St Levan's tower was certainly designed for this purpose: it is in a valley and not even visible from the sea, and yet it is made of good ashlar. There are three **bells** hanging there now:

The **Treble** is 29 inches diameter (73.5 cm) and weighs 5 cwt (226 kg); founder: Abel Rudhall of Gloucester; inscription: "Thomas Robert Bennett Churchwarden ♄ A Ruddle 1754" ♄ was Rudhall's mark (or the nearest my computer could come to it!), and he and his Gloucester family were famous bell-founders from 1684 to 1835, producing over 5,000 bells.

The **Second** is 28¼ inches diameter (72 cm) and weighs 3¾ cwt (170 kg); founder: Mears & Stainbank Whitechapel; inscription: "Cast by Mears & Stainbank 1881." The Whitechapel Bell Foundry is in the *Guinness Book of Records* as Britain's oldest manufacturing company, having been established in 1570; they also cast Big Ben and Philadelphia's Liberty Bell.

The **Tenor** is 33³/₈ inches diameter (85 cm) and weighs 6½ cwt (295 kg); founder: unknown; inscription: "1641." This bell is listed by the Council for the Care of Churches as worthy of preservation.

The **tower** would once have been more evident from inside the church. The internal door, which leads to what is now the vestry and is kept locked, was not there for most of its history. In the far corner of the tower there is a stair-case for the bell-ringers, and at one time also to reach the gallery. The evidence for the use of the gallery is slightly confused: in the late 1860s at least, we know the poor of the parish sat here, those who could not afford to pay for their pews, because the Rector said so at the time in an account of church seating. At about the same time, William Bottrell wrote fancifully of the pew-ends begging "that the ugly gallery, a new thing to them, which hides the beautiful tower arch, makes the nave ugly, and keeps the light from them, may be thrown out of the church without delay. And if the singers must have a gallery… there will be plenty of room for it within the tower."[1] Perhaps the new Rector did throw out the ugly gallery, and consign the poor to the room revealed behind.

At the back of the tower, now completely obscured from the inside by a cupboard, is what remains of the **west door**. In pre-Reformation times, this door was used for processions, especially at Corpus Christi; but after about 1550 processions were banned and the door became surplus to requirements. It was blocked very recently.

The south porch from the interior: Looking out along the path leading to St Levan's Holy Well and Chapel. The ancient Churchyard Cross is just visible to the left of the door. This porch seems to have been built some time after the south aisle and may have replaced an earlier porch over the now disappeared Norman south door.

Either side of the vestry door are **stone tablets**: the Lord's Prayer and the Apostles' Creed, both dated 1849. Their predecessors would have been behind the altar.

The North Wall and the Dairy

Parts of the north wall are Norman. You can make out where the long-blocked-up **north door** stood. Doors are important and interesting in churches, because there were rules about who could use them and when, and indeed how. Even a tiny church like St Levan had at least three doors, and each had its use and users. The south door was for the laity. In some places it was for centuries specifically for the male laity, while the women used the north door. The demolition of the Norman south wall when the south aisle was constructed means that any door there has disappeared – but the Norman arch from the old south door was surely transferred to the 'new' one.

The north door was also the Devil's door. Traditionally the font was placed half-way between the south and north doors: the christening party came and went through the south door, and the north door was left open, so that at the moment of baptism, the Devil could flee through it. On all other occasions, it might be kept locked.

That is not the end of the uses of the north door. Many churches had a picture of St Christopher above this door, so that it could be seen even by those glancing in through the south door: the sight of the patron-saint of travellers protected you from footpads and bandits. There can never have been much passing trade at St Levan Churchtown, and perhaps this saint was not represented here; but it is likely that there was some saint there, to console and help.

The Dairy (north transept) from near the south door, showing the bad fit between the (16th-century) arcade and the (13th-/14th-century) transept. The pillars were planned to reach the length of the church, as on the south side, and to flank a north aisle, replacing the transept. The work was abandoned at the Reformation.

We come now to the **Dairy**, so-called because for many years it was used as such, blocked off from the main part of the church and attached by the church farm (or so the story goes; there is no sign of a door). It seems to have been reclaimed at the time of the 1870s restoration by JD Sedding, one of the best Victorian church architects.

The **arches** across the entrance to the Dairy are very awkwardly placed and many visitors must have wondered at the obstacle. The explanation is that these arches were only the first of what was to have been a series down the length of the church to the west wall, and very probably also through the chancel to the east wall (as on the south). This would have created a processional space: the line, having processed around the outside of the church with its banners and images, would have entered through the west door and then made its way around the inside of the church, using the new side-aisles to make a full circuit. But Henry VIII had other uses for the money, and for the church. The work stopped, for good, and this odd blockage remains.

Inside the Dairy is the **organ**. This was installed as late as 1962, and was made by Henry Speechley & Co of the Camden Organ Factory in London. It replaced a harmonium, as St Levan's first church-organist remembers:

> I do remember a photo in the paper of the new organ being dedicated by the then Bishop, with me sitting primly and proudly aged 16 as the organist – the reason being that when we had the harmonium it involved pedalling really hard to make any noise, and I was the only person who could vaguely play the piano and was young enough to be able to pedal so hard. I also have the original receipt for the "new" organ and it cost £508.

As you may read on the brass plaque on the organ, it is in memory of members of the Talbot family. Not 30 years later, an overhaul of the organ cost the church over twice the purchase price.

The over-restored **lancet windows** are very different from the other windows in the church: they are rather older, dating from perhaps the 14th century.

Looking north here, the memorial immediately to the right is of particular interest – not least because in 1838, a local historian said it was "only object worthy of attention" in the entire church! Our values have changed, but Thomasin Dennis remains interesting. In translation, the text reads:

> Thomasin Dennis of Trembath, born 29th September 1771, of sweet temperament, distinguished by her virtue and most distinguished by her learning, alas! having been slowly but prematurely snatched away by death, died 30th August 1809, aged 38.

Miss Dennis was born in 1771 at Sawah (now Ardensawah, on the lane to Porthgwarra), and later moved to Trembath, just this side of Penzance. She was a clever child, especially proficient in languages, and her modest local fame meant that she became friendly with the family of Josiah Wedgwood (founder of the Wedgwood pottery) when they came to this part of the world. She joined them as a companion and to help with the education of their son, but soon became ill, and had to return home. There she nursed her only sister who had TB; Thomasin died a few years after. None of her poetry was published, but in 1806 her novel *Sophia St. Clare* appeared, and was a failure. A few copies survive: in the British Library, in the Courtney Library in Truro and the Morrab Library in Penzance. Her work is now forgotten.

To the left of the window is a memorial to the longest-serving curate St Levan ever had, from the days when a curate was all the parish did have: James Bevan. He was from Glamorganshire, and was curate of St Levan and Sennen (jointly, as was the practice) for 36 years, dying in 1812. Nearly 20 years later, "in 1831 this tablet was erected by subscription in commemoration of his faithful service." The Revd James clearly made a lasting and good impression on a parish which was often neglected by those charged to care for its spiritual welfare.

Beyond the Thomasin Dennis memorial is one to members of the Roberts family, who were farmers and major landowners in the parish, and provided many churchwardens. Mentions of another important family, the Hodges, can be seen in the slate slabs on the floor just outside the Dairy. The slab partly covered by the pew in the Dairy tells of three Hodge children who died in infancy within 14 months in 1789 and 1790.

11

The Pulpit and Rood Screen

The **pulpit** is interesting: it is of Roman Catholic design, bearing the date 1752, and perhaps brought here a century later. The inscription inside tells us that it was restored in 1930 in memory of BE Weston, another Eastern Telegraph employee. On the wall above the pulpit is a modern bronze sculpture of St Levan and his fishes, the work of local artist Judy Reed, and cast by the Falmouth School of Art and Design.

The dado of the **rood screen** across the entrance to the chancel is largely early Tudor, and is of a piece with the most of the older pew-ends. Together they form the greatest treasure of this church, representing (in the same way as the wall-paintings would have) the images which contributed to and symbolized the beliefs and values of the parish. The Victorian restoration re-created the missing upper half of the screen, which is now on the south side of the chancel (to your right as you face the altar). You can see where the pillars were chipped away to make space for the Rood beam: this may have been done by the Victorians or perhaps they used the original incisions.

The Anglo-Saxon and Norman churches that stood here did not have a rood screen, but in all probability this church did from at least the time the south aisle was built. Sadly, not a single rood screen survives intact in England. (St Buryan has a very fine example, but it contains substantial modern elements.) The purpose of this screen was to support the Rood: i.e., the Cross. In some places, the Rood was painted above the chancel arch, but there is no arch here (though there may well have been one in the Norman church).

The Rood was wooden, and probably had a life-sized Christ figure on it. Such crosses usually both rested on the rood beam and hung from the ceiling. To the left (north) of the cross stood a statue of Mary, mother of Jesus, and to the right a statue of John: "Now there stood by the cross of Jesus his mother… When Jesus saw his mother, and the disciple standing by, whom he loved [i.e. John], he saith unto his mother, Woman, behold thy son!" (John 19:25-26).

Regular access was needed to the Cross: a light was kept there at all times except during Lent, when the whole Rood was shrouded. And so there is a stair up to the rood loft. You can see it in the south wall (and on the outside

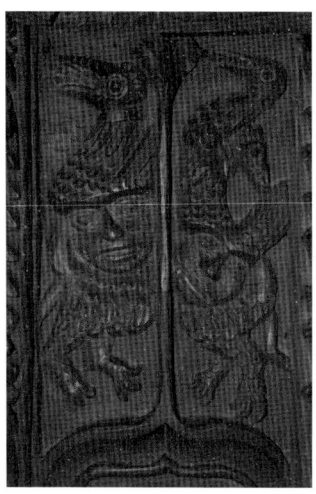

Roodscreen image 1 (*left*): These are assumed to be wyverns, although the feet and heads are rather different from others here. The meaning of the men's faces in their bellies in unknown, as is the reason for one of the monsters having two heads. Perhaps it was all to make them more monstrous.

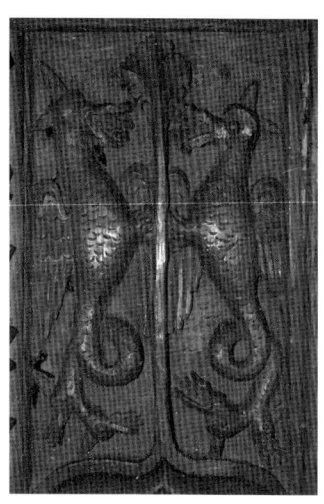

Roodscreen image 2 (*below*): Is this tree growing a crop of wyverns, or is it turning into a wyvern? Are they wyverns at all? All the rood images on this upper plane have a three-leaved tree up the middle, representing perhaps the Tree of Jesse (the ancestry of Christ) or the Trinity.

Roodscreen image 3 (*above*): This is perhaps the clearest representation of the wyvern at St Levan. You can see the two feet (which is what distinguishes the wyvern from the dragon, which has four), and the wings. The tail ends in two further heads, but this is not essential wyvern development. More usually the tail is simply barbed with poison.

Roodscreen image 4 (*right*): Many people think that these are seahorses. Look again! There are feet (two each) and wings: these are wyverns, renowned for their wickedness, and also associated with disease and pestilence. They did not exist.

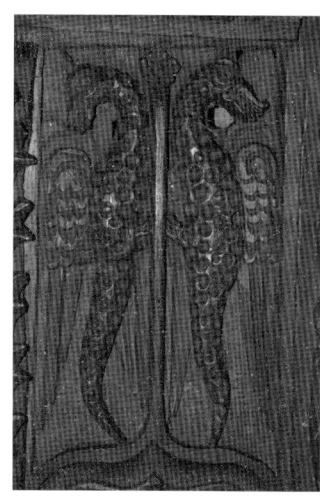

you can see a bulge in the wall to accommodate it). Its dimensions suggest that it was a child's job.

There is a problem, however: how did anyone get from the top of the south-aisle rood screen over to the Rood itself? A pillar is firmly in the way. The best guess is that there was a stair behind where the pulpit is now, which was destroyed in (say) the 1530s, when preparations for the north aisle began, and the Norman pillar which is there now was moved to block it. Once the north aisle was in place, access could have been created from there, with a creep-hole to the central section. But of course the north aisle was never built; and at about the same time, rood screens were banned.

The Images on the Rood Screen

Only the lower part of the rood screen survives, and not all of that. What we have is in two parts, one each side of the access-gap into the chancel. Each side has two bays: there would have been a fifth bay, for the door into the chancel, but that is lost. Also lost is the colouring: for example, some fragments of cresting from the screen were found 75 years ago which show traces of red and gold paint.

There are 36 sections in all, not counting the various edgings (which are well worth examining), and there is not space here to describe them all. Along the bottom are semi-realistic carvings of people, animals and flowers, all similar to, but less detailed than, the old pew-end carvings. In the middle the design is like a shield within a shield, and the inner shield usually displays an important symbol, often an Instrument of the Passion. Above each shield is a carving which, with two exceptions, is of plants or mythological creatures. The whole, including the panel- and bay-borders and the transoms, is elaborately and beautifully executed and is mounted within a modern framework, including a backing to strengthen it.

Some parts are, however, better carved than others: perhaps a master's work as against an apprentice's. Some are in much better condition than others: the result of how they were stored through the many years they were hidden away, maybe, or of the quality of the wood.

The work of reassembling it, about 140 years ago, must have been much like solving a jigsaw but with a creative aspect – if you have time to sit and look closely at it, you can judge whether you would have made a better job of it! Try, for example, the top left-hand corner of the first left-hand bay. And notice that the dividers between panels, all looking like a clutch of notched sticks, are also all different.

To point out just a few of the pictures, starting with the group at the bottom of the panel to the right of the opening into the chancel. The work is simple, but not without expression: a unicorn, a stern man (I think you can see a beard) and a pelican — these are not only charming, but also representative of the eclectic nature of the whole. The unicorn is a fierce mythical beast which can only be captured by a virgin; it is sometimes said to connote Christ, and may have that significance here. The man, if it is a man, may represent a member of the congregation at St Levan when the screen was made, or perhaps it was the carver, or a wholly imagined person. The pelican is not mythical, although the attribute it is displaying here is: it was believed to cut its own breast to provide blood to revive its dead young; and it often represents Christ, who shed his blood for us.

The most beautiful sections are the upper ones, but they are also the least important theologically. They are of two types — wyvern-like beasts and stylized trees; one is both, and another has men's heads emerging out of wyverns' bodies. All have a tree-like stem rising to a tripartite leaf-like design, perhaps a reference to the Trinity, and perhaps also to the Tree of Jesse (which traces Jesus' descent). Wyverns are not as well known as they used to be: they are like dragons but have two legs, rather than four. Nor do they breathe fire, but sometimes they have poisonous stings in their tails. No stings are evident here, but one section (left) shows the tails of the wyverns ending in wyvern-heads.

Last, and most important, are the images in the shields. Five (possibly six) of the twelve are Instruments of the Passion: looking from the left you can see the Flail, the Hammer, the Spear, the Cross and Crown of Thorns, and the Scourging Pillar; there is also a strange blank shield (which was carved to be blank). Four of the shields are very unusual, although at first glance they may look like nails. They could be letters: they could read 'IHC,' a variant on IHS or IHU, all usually with stroke near the 'H' to indicate a contraction and all common mediæval abbreviations for Jesus. It is by no means certain that

 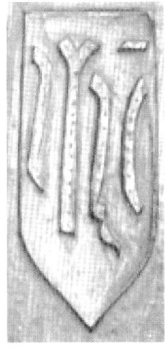 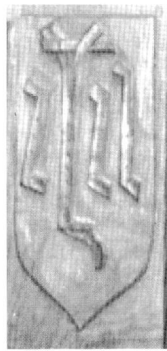 

Christogram: These strange images might be taken to be of the nails from the Cross, but in fact they are almost certainly crude variations on IHS or IHC (the most common variants derived from the first three letters of the Greek name of Jesus).
You can see another such on one of the pew ends. One explanation is that they were executed by an illiterate – but there are two rather fine renditions of a capital 'A' elsewhere in the church (one rood screen panel and one pew-end), so why were these rough carvings permitted to survive?

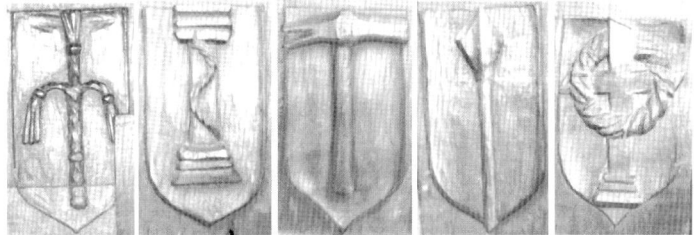

Instruments of the Passion: These are taken from various panels of the roodscreen and show some of the Instruments of the Passion – that is, items associated with Christ's experience immediately before his crucifixion – placed there to help the congregation in their worship. Shown here are (l-r) the Flail (with which Christ was scourged; this panel has been patched, as you can see), the Pillar (where he was scourged), the Hammer (which drove in the nails), the Spear (which pierced Christ's side), and the Crown of Thorns, draped over the cross. Missing altogether from this screen are the Grail and the Titulus Cruci (INRI – the sign affixed to the Cross), both of which may have been on what is now a lost section. Instead, there appears many times in this church the Christogram.

this is what we are looking at, but it is the best guess so far! Perhaps they were simply intended to puzzle.

There is also an elaborate letter 'A' (a far cry from the IHS carvings!), which may be the initial of a benefactor, and another mythical beast, this time a manticore. This fellow is out of place – he should surely be up with the wyverns – but here he is, a man's face on a lion's body with the tail of a scorpion and the wings of an angel. Manticores also have two or three rows of teeth, not visible here.

The Chancel

Much of the furniture in the chancel has been given in memory of people who obviously loved St Levan. The chair is *in memoriam* William Henry Dodge MRCS, who died in 1904. Although he retired to St Austell, for many years he was living in Penzance and working as a doctor. He will have known this church from the time when it was a dilapidated survivor of the neglect of the last Dean.

The desk to the right is *in memoriam* Jane Troughton Borlase, in 1912. The altar rail is in memory Alfred Izard (1893-1963) and his wife Bessie (1904-1988), whose family funded its purchase.

All the paintings which would have graced the mediæval walls, both here and in the nave, have long since been painted over, and we have little notion of what they might have shown. In 1877, during the restoration, the whole interior was re-plastered, and in 1997, this plaster failed and had itself to be replaced. In the course of this work, two **niches** were found which you can now see in the north wall of the sanctuary, to the left of the altar. Their existence had been quite unsuspected, and their use is not certain. The large niche was probably a 12th-century window, and perhaps later an aumbry (i.e., a cupboard for storing sacred objects, such as the chrism oil and the altar vessels): the north wall is the usual place for one. The purpose and date of the niche nearest to the east wall remain unknown; perhaps it was also an aumbry.

The lowest niche, with the ogee arch, has never been covered up. It was once the **piscina** (i.e., a basin for washing sacred vessels), and was on the south wall. It was removed to make room for the late 19th-century piscina in current use – which presumably uses the ancient drain would have led from

Detail of one of the altar frontals: This beautiful piece was purchased for the church about 50 years ago (from a catalogue, as far as is known), and is St Levan's Festive Frontal. Different frontals are used on the chancel altar at different times of the liturgical year, the colour varying according to season. This detail has also been weaved into the cover design of this book.

the basins to the sanctified ground. The date of the 'north' piscina is probably early 15th-century.

The oak **reredos,** which was behind the altar in 1880 or so has been removed, in part to expose ancient features of the church. St Levan's architect at the time wanted to expose "the remains of the sill and jambs of the original 13th-century window and the marks of the Reredos subsequently added in Mediæval times" – and they can be made out. The carved stone frieze which is where the reredos was is of a piece with the modern piscina, and probably dates from the same time. The **piscina**, with an ogee arch like its predecessor, has a credence shelf.

The **altar** table is of wood and is enclosed on three sides. The original altar was almost definitely made of stone, and may well have sheltered relics of Selevan (St Levan); stone altars were ordered to be destroyed at the Reformation, and instead, wooden tables were set in the nave. This altar table is most likely of a later date, perhaps from the time of the Victorian restoration.

The **east window** is Victorian stained glass: St Peter is on the left, holding the keys of heaven, and St John is on the right, holding a book (for his gospel) and a chalice (one legend says that he drank from a poisoned chalice and was unharmed); in the centre is Jesus holding a baby, with the words underneath "Suffer the little children to come unto me" (Luke 18:16).

The crucifix is believed to be of Italian make, and may have been part of the gift from Mrs. Blaber, who presented the church with the **sanctuary lamp** which hangs to one side of the chancel. This is silver, of Italian design, and according to the church records had been given to Mrs. Blaber's mother, Lady Walsingham, by the Princess de Teano. This was Vittoria Colonna (1880-1954), a great beauty in her day, and distantly related to Mrs. Blaber; their connexion with St Levan is not known.

The Lady Chapel

The **Lady Chapel**, at the east end of the south aisle, is a 20th-century creation. There is no sign of its having been a chapel before the 19th century, though that does not mean that was not. It may, for example, have been used by a pre-Reformation parish guild.

Some records indicate that in the 19th century it was called the Mortuary Chapel; presumably funerals were conducted here, and the intention was that memorials be erected here. In 1866, Mrs. Hodge offered to give £150 to renovate it in memory of her husband, and this was gratefully accepted, but later references seem to indicate that the money was spent on the chancel instead – which, given the poor state of the whole building at that time, was surely a priority. A plan from the 1870s shows the harmonium against the east wall here, with the player facing north, and seating to his left facing the same way, presumably for the choir.

Be that as it may, it was not until the 1930s that what is now

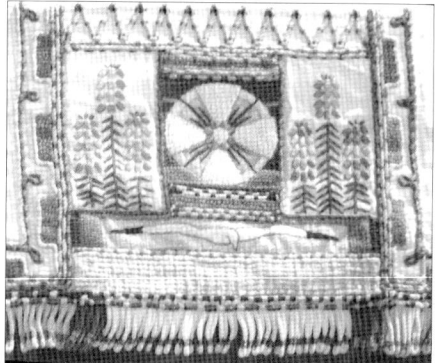

Detail of the Lady Chapel altar frontal: The cloth was designed and embroidered by Rowena Cade, the founder of the Minack Theatre and benefactor of St Levan church. (See the south window in the Lady Chapel, and the pew-ends dedicated to her sister and brother-in-law – 31 and 32 on the pew plan.) The Minack is about a kilometre away along the cliffs, on the Coast Path.

the Lady Chapel was refurbished. The single oak bench which had been there for the use of the (non-existent) choir was incorporated into the new Delabole-slate floor, along with two old slate panels on which are carved the **Ten Commandments**. In 1561, an Order from Elizabeth I had required that in all churches "there be fixed upon the wall, over the said communion board, the tables of God's precepts imprinted for the said purpose": these tables in the Lady Chapel floor are presumably copies of the Elizabethan ones. This work is dated 1777.

The **parclose screen** on the north side of the chapel is Victorian in its upper half and 1930s in the lower. The upper part was, as mentioned, removed from the rood screen, partly to leave the screen as far as possible original, and partly to create this partition. The lower part has an inscription in Cornish along its length:

Rag carensa dew ha rag cov sans selevan cryst agan bara terrys ragon ny.

(For love of God, and in memory of St Selevan,
Christ our bread broken for us.)

There is no record of who made this. For the **stained-glass window** on the south wall of the Chapel, see the picture on page 83. The chair here commemorates Winifred Bamford, who died in 1940 aged 38.

Pew-ends

At last we arrive at the **pew-ends**, the jewels of St Levan. Pews were a relatively late addition to the amenities of a church. The first church seating was for the clergy, who were often in church for long hours: older men were provided with misericords and sediliæ on which to rest. The laity did not have long sermons to hear; they came to pray and to witness mass. If they couldn't stand or kneel, then they sat on the floor. After a time, however, it became more common to place stone benches around the walls and then, gradually, simple wooden benches appeared across the nave. Perhaps the old bench which is now part of the flooring in the Lady Chapel was a survivor of this era.

By the mid-15th century, pews were widespread and the practice of buying the right to use them was increasing. The older pew-ends here at St Levan date from the early 16th century, with the exception of the pew-ends **13** and **19**, which may be 200 years older (and which do not abut seats). Note that none of the seats on these older pews are as old as their ends – and that in fact most of these ends have modern surrounds (**18** is a fine example which does not).

If you been following the order of this Guide, then you will be coming out of the Lady Chapel: on your left the first two pew ends are **32** and **31** on the Plan. These are dedicated to Katharine and Beaufort Burdekin.

Mrs Burdekin (1896-1963) was born Katharine Penelope Cade, the youngest sister of Rowena Cade (of Minack theatre fame). Katharine was a novelist who published under the names Kay

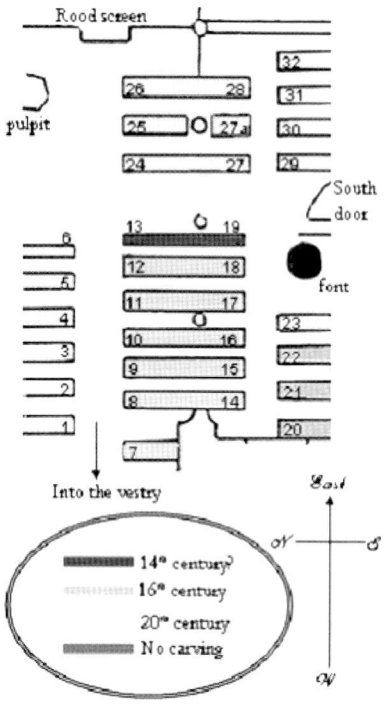

Pew-Plan

Burdekine and Murray Constantine. Her best known book was *Swastika Night*, a science-fiction tale about the evils of fascism set 700 years into the future, which she wrote in 1937; it is still in print. Her pew-end shows flowers and a candle. Her husband, Beaufort Burdekin (1892-1962), was a lawyer, but better known in his day as the winner of a silver medal at the 1912 Olympics in Stockholm: he was a member of the British rowing eight. His pew-end has the Scales of Justice and rowing oars, as well as a seahorse with an anchor.

Across from this, no. **28** on the Plan, is one of two memorial pew-ends to Edward Vernon Molyneux Favell (1917-1944), both rich in references to his life. For example, the upper section shows the coats of arms of Winchester College and of Trinity College Cambridge, both of which he attended. The other end of the pew (**26**) shows the badge of the Oxfordshire and Buckinghamshire Light Infantry, and lower down a Pegasus, the badge of the Airborne Division. The three scallop shells represent pilgrimage.

The Santiago Pilgrim *(17 in the pew-plan)*: My favourite. You can believe that he walked all the way to Santiago de Compostela, in north-west Spain – as English pilgrims did from at least 1100. He may have taken ship from Penzance to Brittany, or gone across the Bay of Biscay to Ferrol or La Coruña; either way, it was a dangerous undertaking, and he looks suitably weary, and content.

Facing Heads *(11 in the pew-plan)*: This pair may well have been apprentice work, and we can only hope the woodworker improved with practice … It was certainly not carved by the master who created the Pilgrim (17) or the Jolly Fool (14). There is another bench-end with male and female heads facing (18), where the man's head is made of decorative swirls.

The Jolly Fool *(14 in the pew-plan):* The use of the Fool in churches at this time may be a learned reference to Erasmus's Praise of Folly (1509): "…all Christian religion seems to have a kind of alliance with folly and in no respect to have any accord with wisdom" – and so on. On the other hand, it may be referring to a verse in at least two Psalms: "The fool says in his heart, there is no God."

The Grim Fool *(8 in the pew-plan):* This one is a puzzle, like many of the carvings here. He looks less sinister in photographs than in 'real life,' where his smile has the quality of a rictus. His hat ends in a cockerel's head, and he carries a staff which is a parody of a bishop's crosier, with a horse- or ass-shoe at its top. He could be a Mock Bishop, but they are usually boys, elected at the New Year as part of the topsy-turvy regime, and this gentleman doesn't fit that bill. Compare him with the much jollier Fool above.

These are also an echo of **17**, one of the best old carvings: he is a pilgrim. The scallop shell on his hat signifies that he has been to Santiago de Compostela, and he is carrying a book, which suggests that he may be a cleric. His weary traveller's face is full of character; perhaps he was a native of St Levan.

Another favourite is at **14**, the fool, with his cap and bells and ass's ears, the accepted "uniform" of the court jester. This figure may have been someone attached to a local grand family; it may be a reference to the fool in the congregation who mocks the proceedings; or it may be simply a comic picture.

The man at **8** (the other end of that bench) at first sight also looks like a fool; but he is not smiling; indeed he looks rather menacing. Perhaps he is fool, but a grim one, a reminder of the plague. JD Sedding thought he was simply a shepherd.

Pew-ends **9** and **16** carry Instruments of the Passion: on **9** there is a saltire (St Andrew's cross), and a cross with the crown of thorns; on **16**, as well as the seamless garment and the dice, the strange lettering seen on the rood screen appears again. Very sophisticated capitals are on ends **10** (an elaborate I [?] and an M), **12** (S, and a letter so elaborate it is indecipherable), and **13** (an A – which may be part of an alpha

St Levan's Fishes (*7 in the pew-plan*): This may be the most precious pew-end in the church, because it is the only surviving pre-Reformation reference to Selevan (for the story of Selevan and the fishes, see p. 34). We can imagine preachers down the centuries keeping the tale alive by pointing to this carving. You will note that there are only two fishes, not three as in the modern carving behind the pulpit: two is correct.

and omega). The 'A' on this last echoes the 'A' on the roodscreen, and may well refer to the same person. And there are wyverns again too: a pair of wyverns at **19**, and what could be a wyvern's head at the end of the young man's cap at **15**. Selevan's fishes are at **7**, possibly the oldest reference we have to the legend, which is undoubtedly older than that.

One of the Favell memorials *(26 in the pew-plan)*: There are two modern pew-ends in memory of EVM Favell (1917-44). This one shows the badge of the Oxfordshire and Buckinghamshire Light Infantry and, lower down, the badge of the Airborne Division, a Pegasus. The three scallop shells represent pilgrimage (and are perhaps also a reminder of the Pilgrim at pew-end no 17); the IHS and chi-rho at the base mean, respectively, "Jesus Hominum Salvator" (Jesus Saviour of Man) and "Christ" (as it consists of the first two letters of 'Christ' in Greek).

Alpha and Omega *(13 in the pew-plan)*: There is general agreement that this is an Alpha and Omega (the first and last letters of the Greek alphabet), which in this context is a reference to the verse in Revelations 1: "I am Alpha and Omega, the first and the last." However, the omega does not look like any other known example (except for the modern copy across the aisle from this one!). Within the 'omega' is the sacred heart: Jesus's heart, expressing the divine love for humanity.

Outside the Church

The Sundial

This is a well-made dial, carved on slate, as is common, but rather taller and narrower than is usual. The maker and date are unknown, but it could well be mid-18th century like St Buryan's and others in West Penwith.

The Churchyard Cross

The Cross is regarded as one of the finest examples of its type in Cornwall. It is over 2 metres tall (7 ft) and is decorated on all four sides, although the healthy lichen means that much of the patterning is now obscured. The face towards the path has a crucified Christ figure, with three panels below decorated with diagonal lines, while the face towards the Stone has an equal-armed cross, the bottom arm of which extends to the foot of the Cross. The edges on both faces are beaded, and the sides are carved with geometric patterns.

A Tour of the Exterior

Now walk clockwise around the church. The cross on the Favell grave, lichen-smothered and ancient-looking, is in fact modern. You can see the blocked western door at the foot of the tower: this was done very recently in order to create the vestry. The tower is original, except for the window above this door, which is a Victorian copy.

Continuing round to the north side of the church, the outline of the old north door is much more visible than it is from the inside. You can also see one of the coffin rests on your left, with a stone-built cattle grid to keep the beasts out of the graveyard. This was at the end of the churchpath from Ardensawah and Bosistow. Straight ahead at this point is the other coffin rest, up a long flight of steps and itself at the foot of a steep field path northwards to Trengothal and Trebehor, with a branch from Raftra, and eastwards to Rospletha. Trengothal is over two miles away, so the coffin-rest must have been a very welcome sight!

Next to this latter coffin-rest is a wayside cross, thought to be a late-mediæval copy of the cross on the back of the Churchyard Cross. The carved block of stone underneath recorded the names of the churchwardens who caused the rest to be placed here: it is illegible now. In the hedge opposite this Cross, there is a carved stone with what was once clearly a headless figure, which may have been part of a crucified Christ. However, not everyone agrees that it is from a cross, and in its present position, where it is hard to see even the front (and the back is quite invisible), it is not possible to say with certainty.

In coming from one coffin-rest to the other, you passed the Dairy – the north transept – one of the older parts of the church still largely visible: perhaps 14th-century like the tower. It is said to have been annexed for agricultural use at some point (perhaps during the Civil War) and was only restored to the church much later, perhaps when the whole was refurbished by JD Stedding in the 1870s. There is no sign of access to the Dairy other than through the church itself.

It is hard to tell how far the way the church nestles into its site is due to the natural slope of the ground and how far to the rise in level of the churchyard because of the number of burials over the centuries: Charles Thomas estimates that "something like 2 metres has been vertically added since Norman times." It certainly enhances the impression which St Levan gives of being a hidden gem.

On the south side of the church you can see the bulge in the wall which accommodates the rood steps. It seems to have been an after-thought: the space for the steps was thus made after the south aisle was built – but not very long after!

St Levan's Stone

The split stone in the churchyard, behind the Churchyard Cross, was almost certainly a pre-Christian site, most likely the central motif of a female fertility cult (see p. 36); it is unusual to find pagan relics so near a church. It has been suggested that it is simply some unworked moorstone left behind by the 16th-century builders when the north aisle was abandoned (see p. 55), but the split looks natural, and there is no sign of its ever having been anywhere but here. Stones of this kind have been worshipped in many places in the world: the

The sundial over the south porch: A fine example of a simple sundial, this one is nearly half an hour fast, which may be because a wedge was left out when it was re-hung. There is some packing visible, a failed attempt to get the angle right. The words "Sicut Umbra transeunt Dies" mean "The days pass like shadows."

The Cross and inscription by the eastern coffin rest: This round cross-head almost certainly once crowned a much longer shaft. The inscription on the stone commemorates the churchwardens of 1794, William Hodge and William Mitchell, who presumably caused work to be done to the coffin-rest. Perhaps they arranged for it to be built. The church path here leads north to Trebehor and Trengothal and east to Rospletha and St Buryan.

The main Churchyard Cross: Of the many fine Anglo-Saxon crosses in West Penwith, St Levan's stands out. In the late mediæval period, the Cross would have been an important part of religious processions in the parish, perhaps a starting point. Its position should be understood in relation to the Stone, and also perhaps to the Anglo-Saxon church (see p. 25). The consensus is that the Cross stands where it has always stood.

St Levan's Stone: A rare example of a pagan monument on sanctified ground. The wonderful Churchyard Cross is just out of the picture to the left. This picture also shows the superior stone in which the tower was built: this is the usual practice, because the structure has to bear the weight of the bells.

St Levan Scrapbook has a photograph of a very similar stone in the Chamba region of the Himalayas, reportedly with a trident stamped on it – which may be Shiva claiming the female form for his own, or Parvati claiming it for herself (they both wield tridents). Similar comments have been made about the siting of the Cross near the Stone (see p. 39).

There is a famous legend about the Stone (see p. 36), but there is no indication that the split is widening. If St Levan's Chapel (see below) is indeed the first Christian church here, it is noteworthy that it was not built near the Stone; equally important is the fact that at some later stage it was decided that the church should be set up in direct competition, so to speak.

Holy Well

The Holy Well is beside the footpath from the Churchtown to Porth Chapel, and not far from the Chapel further down the cliff. It was badly restored in the 1980s, but has been more sensitively re-pointed recently. When Dr Borlase, who was the first to record it, saw it in the mid-18th century, it had a roof still, but that is long gone. The stone is undressed and there is nothing to help date the structure: in fact, as Charles Thomas has said, "the walling most resembles a Cornish hedge."

St Levan's Chapel

The route to the Chapel from the Well is down a flight of stone steps, which until 1931 had been hidden for many years. The Revd H T Valentine and Dr Vernon Favell excavated them, and they have remained in use until today.

It is a double-celled structure, the easternmost being regarded as the chapel and the western section as possibly a hermit's dwelling. The chapel is about 6 ft by 12 and the living cell about 6 ft by 9. It may be the oldest Christian building in Cornwall, but it is not possible to be sure. (See also p. 38 below.)

St Levan's Holy Well: There was at least one holy well in virtually every parish in Penwith, some of them still worth a visit – for example at Madron, the two at Sancreed, Alsia – but none has the magnificent setting of St Levan, which these photographs illustrate. The well building is an otherwise unimpressive ruin, but its history and its position guarantee it a following still. (See also the picture on p. 38.)

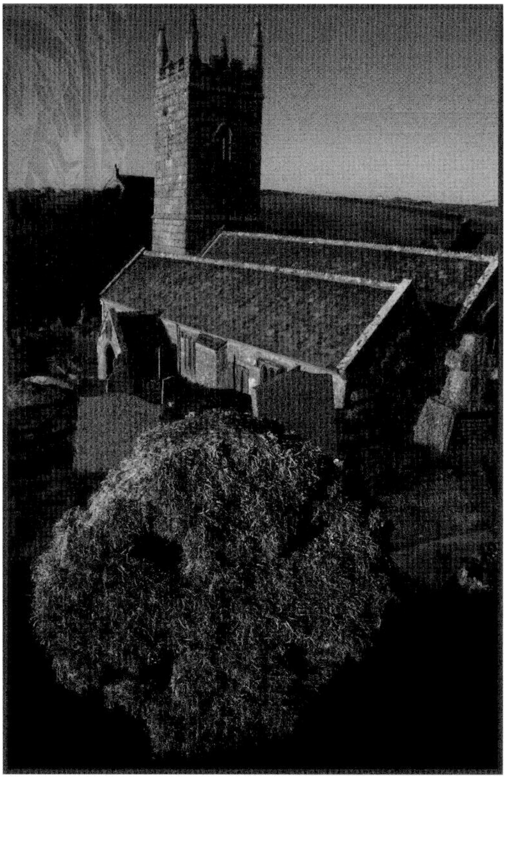

Part Two

The History of St Levan and his Church

The earliest surviving mention of St Levan parish (and by implication its church) is in the lay subsidy rolls of 1327,[2] but then for several hundred years there are only fleeting allusions to it as part of the Deanery of St Buryan. The parish registers survive from 1694,[3] but it is only in 1864, when St Levan became an independent parish with its own Rector, that the full life of the church comes into view.

This short history, by setting out a summary of what is known about the church, will help to explain why St Levan was so ill-served. It will also discuss what little is known about the saint to whom it is dedicated.

Christianity comes to West Penwith

When did Christianity come to West Cornwall? No one knows. It was the Romans, who were in occupation of Britain between about 50 and 400AD, who first brought Christianity to Britain, but they were not very high-profile in Cornwall. Cornwall, as so often in its history, was on the margins. Roman Christians may well have traded here, or have been among the soldiers who passed through; but as to whether any practicing Christians settled here before the Roman authority left these shores, we will probably never be able to say. It is possible that Christianity in Penwith was purely post-Roman, but by about 550, the Cornish were Christian "at least in a nominal sense."[4] No one really knows how this happened either.

Cornish saints played a rather different cultural and religious rôle from the Catholic tradition of martyrs, great teachers and exceptionally holy people who were able to work miracles in life and beyond. This seems to be at least partly because the Christianity of Cornwall, Wales and Brittany was isolated for several crucial centuries while Roman Catholic ideas of sainthood and cults spread through the rest of western Europe. The Romans rarely ventured this far west and although the Anglo-Saxons eventually conquered the peninsula, they had been repulsed several times over the centuries. By the time their invasion succeeded, in the 10th century, the character of Cornish Christianity had settled into a different pattern:

> Cornwall, in contrast [to Devon and the rest of England], has retained large numbers of church buildings dedicated to local Celtic saints, and for a long time extramural places of worship were important: wells, trees, paths, rocks and islands.[5]

For the rest, Celtic Christianity appears to have been a matter of shared belief and ritual, revolving around baptism, communion and burial, and support for the priesthood. These holy men (women saints were not priests) and their followers have been called monks, but this does not mean that they were members of any recognized monastic order. There were no books laying down the rules to be obeyed, but they were expected to be ascetics, and they were usually scholars of a sort and nearly always teachers. They would look strange to us, with their heavy beards, their hair "shaved in front of a line drawn from ear to ear, the hair hanging down long behind."[6]

We would not mistake them for the vicar. One of them (perhaps) was the man we call St Levan.

Selevan, aka St Levan
The name

The first known mention of Selevan: This is a tracing of an image in a 10th-century Vatican document, which lists other local saints, like 'Berion' (Buryan). The name above is not 'Levan': one thing we know for certain about St Levan is that he was not called Levan. In this document he is called *Salamun* — that is, *Solomon*; the Welsh is *Selim*, or *Selyf*, or *Selyv*, and the Irish is *Sullivan*.

At left is the first definite reference to 'our' saint. It is from a document which is now in the Vatican, a list of saints written in about 900AD, most probably in Brittany.[7] Selevan, it would seem (see caption), was just one version of a familiar name.[8]

The next written evidence of his name is in 1327 and 1340, when official documents refer to his church as the *Parochia Sancti Silvani*.[9] 'Silvanus' was used for quite some time in official documents of the later mediæval period. Some Penwith Hundred court rolls of c1469 refer to *Siluan*, in a list next to Berian and Senen:[10] perhaps an Englishing of *Silvanus*. The consensus is that 'Silvanus' was an attempt to make sense of the Cornish *Selevan*: this vernacular version was first noted in 1545[11], but it is thought to be far older. '*Slevan*' remains the local pronunciation.

The Cornish used the Christian names only of their saints, and the addition of 'Saint' was an English usage: the corruption of Selevan into St Levan seems a prime example of this:[12] so Anglo-Saxon ears, accustomed to 'Saint' before a saint's name, heard 'St Levan' instead of 'Slevan.' As far as surviving records are concerned, '*St Levan*' makes its début as the name of the place on Saxton's 1574 map of Cornwall.[13] Another cartographer heard differently: John Speed's 1610 map of Cornwall has *Sleven*.[14] As late as 1763 there is a reference to *Sellan*.[15] St Levan as the *saint's* name (as opposed to the place-name) does not appear in print until the 18th century,[16] while in 19th-century sources you can find St *Livin* and *Leven*.

I shall call him Selevan.

There are those who say that the Selus Stone in the church at St Just-in-Penwith is Selevan's grave marker, but the date of the stone (estimated by some to be fourth or fifth century) may be far too early;[17] and in any case, as far as we know he has always been very closely associated with what is now St Levan and its border with St Buryan. Why would his tomb be in St Just?

The topography

There are a few places in the area whose names may contain some memory of where Selevan lived or was at least known. For example, Bosliven was formerly 'Bosselyvyn', which means the house of Selevan and (although not everyone agrees[18]) this may be a reference to the saint. Bodellan, a former farm on the edges of what is now Porthcurno, has long been spoken of as Selevan's home, and is also a 'bos' term. All its historical forms are pretty much the same and give no clue to its original meaning[19] – but it may (just) be a corruption of bos-slevan.

Porthleven, on the east side of Mount's Bay close to Helston, is not named for Selevan: the saint there is Elvan.

So far, so unsatisfactory. What we are left with is legend.

The Legends

"They are but poor petrified things, these legends of later date," wrote a late-19th-century historian, and she was right.[20] Here they are anyway.

Tradition has it that Selevan lived near Bodellan, an ancient farm at the edge of Porthcurno. From there he walked daily to Porth Chapel (the beach below St Levan Church) along a path whose grass grew greener under his foot – as the grass is said to have done under the foot of St Paul Aurelian at nearby Paul.[21] Selevan was a great fisherman, and the second-best-known tale about him revolves around this and a visit his sister and her children made to him at Bodellan. There are at least two versions of this story extant: one has the saint catching two bream (also known as chad) on one hook, and throwing them back into the sea – Selevan was "anxious to serve both alike,"[22] only to catch them again a second and then a third time. This last time he decided that he ought to keep them, and he took them home, only to find his sister St Breage waiting for him with her children. (Sometimes the sister is called Manaccan.) Selevan prepared the fish for their supper, but the children were so hungry they gobbled the food and choked to death on it.

The variant on this is in Jeffery Burr's *History of the Church of St Levan*, in which Selevan knows he has guests when he goes out to fish for supper. His explanation of the grisly end is that

> St Levan looked upon this as punishment for his dissatisfaction in not accepting the first fish, the gift of food from God. From that time onwards the fishermen of Land's End district called the chad 'chuck-cheeld' or 'choke child'.[23]

Dissatisfaction with the food God gives is obviously central to the sin here, but why did the innocent children die rather than Selevan? (Not to mention why people were using Anglo-Saxon words hundreds of years before the Anglo-Saxons came to West Penwith and even more hundreds of years before they stopped speaking Cornish!)

A clue to the tale may lie in two other, less corrupted, stories. The first is about Petroc, who like several saints, was "transported without oar or rower" across the seas "to a certain island". He stayed there for seven years, "fed from time to time with a single fish divinely placed before him at opportune hours:" it was the same fish every time.²⁴

The second is about Neot, another Cornish saint who, like Selevan, caught a fish a day to sustain him (Neot from a well, Selevan from the sea). In Neot's case, this was explicitly a pact with God, and when he fell ill and his servant ignorantly took two fishes from the well, Neot rose from his sickbed and prayed earnestly for forgiveness for his greed. The servant was able to return one fish to the well, where it miraculously came alive once more.²⁵ This suggests that the first version of the Selevan story is closer to the original: we perhaps should understand that Selevan threw the fish back into the sea because he had agreed with God to catch only one a day, and not knowing about his sister's family visiting, he had no reason to take two on this occasion. The death of the children remains a puzzle.

Another tale of Selevan also shows us how these stories have survived:

> Dr Borlase graphically records his visit to the church of St Levan in or about the year 1740. 'Whilst we were at dinner at the inn,' he says, 'it was very pleasant to hear the good old woman, our Landlady, talk of St Levin, his cursing the name Johannah, his taking the same two fishes twice following, his entertaining his sister Manaccan, and as a confirmation of everything we were desir'd upon our departure to observe his walk, the stone he fish'd upon, with some other particularities of like importance.'²⁶

The curse on the name Johannah is a tale quickly told: on his walk from Bodellan to fish at Porth Chapel one Sunday, the saint passed the garden of a woman called Johannah, at Rospletha (the farm on the other side of the road from the entrance to the Minack Theatre). She was picking vegetables for her meal, and chastised Selevan for fishing on a Sunday; he chastised her for accusing him of sinning when she was doing the same as he was about to do: getting dinner. The upshot was that he pronounced that if another Johannah were christened in his church or at his well, the child would grow to be an even greater fool than she was.

A search of the St Levan baptism register (which begins in 1694) reveals only one Johanna and one Joanna. Johanna Hodge was born in 1820; Joanna

Osborne was born in 1837. Even if it is true that St Levan families wishing to call their daughters Jo(h)anna took them to Sennen for baptism, it has to be said that Jo(h)anna was not a very common name anywhere in the Deanery.[27]

The most famous legend concerns St Levan's Stone, which stands in the churchyard. It is a large boulder divided in two. Selevan is reputed to have split the stone with his staff (or possibly with his fist), saying:

> *When with panniers astride*
> *A pack horse can ride*
> *Through St Levan Stone*
> *The World will be done.*

Is it widening? Dr. Borlase was told in 1740 that a generation before "there was scarce room enough to thrust the hand betwixt the parts of this stone, but they are now a foot distance from one to the other." It does not seem to have moved much since then.

St Levan's Stone: Stones of this kind have been worshipped in many places in the world: the St Levan Scrapbook has a photograph of a very similar stone in the Chamba region of the Himalayas, reportedly with a trident stamped on it — which may be Shiva claiming the female form for his own, or Parvati claiming it for herself (they both wield tridents).

Why Selevan should have split the stone in the first place is not known. One suggestion is that it was so that we would remember him (so that worked!). The stone may have other significance, which is discussed later. (See page 39.)

Selevan's Family

Like many Cornish saints, Selevan has been given an aristocratic lineage. In this case, however, there is a much stronger Cornish connexion than is usual. Although he had close ties to Wales – by at least one account, his wife was St Gwen of Wales, and was St David's aunt – in his direct male line, he is Cornish (or Dumnonian) for several generations.

These legends should of course be taken with a huge pinch of salt: for example, one source says that Cybi (Selevan's son) was a friend of St Hilary of Poitiers and that Selevan was a captain of the guard. Now St Hilary lived from about 315 to about 368, and this is far too early given for Cybi to have been his friend.

To sum up so far: there may have been a greatly revered holy man who lived near this church, who may have been called Selevan/Salamun. (On the other hand, Selevan may have been a local nobleman who paid for a church there, or who was buried there.) Various stories have been attached to him, and various versions of his genealogy have survived. What in them represents the truth of the matter is unknown and perhaps unknowable – except that Selevan, whoever he was, has maintained an extraordinary grip on the loyalty and imagination of the people of his parish:

> … although History can tell us little about S Selevan, his memory has been preserved in local legend in a very remarkable way. In only one other parish in Cornwall – that of S Neot – has the story of the local saint been so cherished by the people.[28]

✠ ✠ ✠ ✠ ✠

The beginnings of St Levan Church

The Chapel

It is notoriously hard to date plain stone buildings like the so-called chapel, although there is no doubt that it is old. No one knows when it was built, and the absence of any carving on the stones that remain has suggested to some that it was not a sacred place at all – but it is hard to see what it was if it was not a chapel. Until the 20th century few people chose to live in such exposed places – except of course hermits. It was a two-celled building: this is how many, probably most, mediæval parish churches and chapels began,[29] although perhaps Selevan (or another monk or hermit) lived in the western room, with only the eastern room as a chapel. In the absence of any other evidence, it is reasonable to view this as the first Christian church in St Levan.

At some point during the following four or five hundred years, it was decided to move slightly inland, to where the church now stands – still a secluded spot, but far easier to reach than the cliff-top places, which may well be why the move was made.

A Pagan Site?

The Stone

One question which often occurs to visitors, especially as they look at the large split rock outside the church porch, is whether St Levan was built on a pagan site. Indeed, many people assume that *most* Christian churches were built on pagan sites. However, while there are some apparent instances of Christian co-option of British

ST. LEVAN'S WELL.

St Levan's Holy Well: It is difficult to capture what the Well must once have been like. This drawing, by JT Blight in the mid-19th century, is better than most photographs, perhaps because the building has deteriorated even more since then. Water from the Well is still sometimes used for baptisms, but it was also believed to cure toothache and eye diseases. Sleeping at the Well increased the chances of a cure: given that it is hardly a metre square inside, it would not have been a comfortable night! *(Courtesy of Porthcurno Telegraph Museum)* pagan sites (for example the standing stones at Rudston in Yorkshire and at St Michael's at Awliscombe in Devon), they are rare[30] – as is St Levan's Stone. The position of the very fine St Levan Churchyard Cross relative to the Stone must be deliberate, and looks like an attempt to overcome the Stone's female power. If this is so, the fact that the Stone is still there is either a tribute to its enduring power in the minds of St Levan's parishioners over many centuries, or simply an indication of how completely some stories can be lost.

The Well

The propinquity of churches and wells is remarkable, and not only in remote places. The high altar at Winchester Cathedral is built over a holy well in the crypt; there are two in York Minster; St Mungo's in Glasgow is in the wall of the cathedral. And so on. While there is evidence that such wells have been forgotten in large parts of the country, that is hardly true of Cornwall. Within the small compass of the West Penwith peninsula alone, one can – or could – find at least one holy well in virtually every parish including St Levan.[31]

Christian rituals require water for baptism and for priests to clean the sacramental vessels, and a handy source of water has always been desirable when seeking a place to build a house. So while Selevan may have had the well pointed out to him by local people who knew it as a pagan shrine, the choice of its environs for his chapel also had other reasons.

An intriguing opening in a Raftra wall: Is the door to the church the Devil wanted built at Raftra? Although this picture was taken inside the tractor shed, it has been suggested that we are looking at what was the external wall; it has also been suggested that this was a garden wall. Few believe the chapel theory.

The Devil

There is a surprising number of stories in which the Devil objects to a church's being built where the priest, or lord, or villagers wanted it to be built: overnight he tears the day's work down and transports the stones to his favoured site. There are many examples of such tales (e.g., All Saints Church in Godshill on the Isle of Wight; Napton Church in Warwickshire; and Staple Fitzpaine, near Taunton), and their commonness has led to theories about their meaning. The Devil battling with church-builders is usually seen as an indicator of a pre-Christian holy site – pagans being seen as devil-worshippers – but it is odd that in some stories the church is built where the Devil wants it to be (as at Napton) and in some it is not (as at Staple Fitzpaine). It is also odd that there seem to have been no consequential problems for those churches built on the Devil's choice of site.

The point here is to introduce a little-known St Levan Devil story. Apparently, the Devil was so annoyed at his failure to prevent the church being built at the Churchtown that he built the old 'manor-house' at Raftra instead. Raftra, a farming hamlet almost exactly a kilometre north of the church, is visible from the churchyard, and the farm-house on the southern side of the group (called a manor-house although there is no evidence that it ever was) is one of the oldest buildings in the parish. This seems to be a version of the story outlined above: that the Devil wanted the church built at Raftra, either because Raftra was a pagan site or because the Churchtown was one, and having failed to achieve this, built a beautiful secular building instead.

I was told this story when I was at Raftra to look at an old wall which is said to be part of a ruined chapel. Its claim to authenticity is a Gothic-type door set low in the wall (picture on previous page): it *may* be all that remains of a pre-Reformation chapel. If it is, it could be connected to the story about the Devil and the parish church, and indeed the story could be an explanation of these ruins rather than of the 'manor-house.'

Summary

So is St Levan Church built on pagan ground?
The evidence for this is: a continuity of population and culture; the siting of the original Chapel by the holy well; the St Levan Stone; and the garbled tale about the Devil at Raftra. A major problem in settling the matter is that no one knows what a pagan shrine would have looked like. The descriptions we have tend to be vague – a grove, a well, a rock – and do not give us much help

in identifying this or that site as a pre-Christian place of worship. The main indicator of a pagan past is the Stone – a very persuasive indicator – but the significance of even this is queried. Joanna Mattingly has suggested – perhaps not entirely seriously – that it is merely a semi-worked piece of moorstone, a leftover from the late-mediæval rebuilding which, as we shall see, was abandoned at about the time Henry VIII abandoned Rome.

So, while there is strong evidence, there is no proof, that St Levan Church was built on a site with strong pagan associations. At this stage of knowledge, nothing more can be said.

St Levan's Shrine

If very little is known of Selevan and the early years of Christianity in St Levan, the following centuries are not much better. It is certain that there was a shrine to Selevan here, because mediæval churches always had shrines to the saint to whom they were dedicated. Given that this was Selevan's home-town, so to speak, there will have been numerous relics associated with him and his ministry. The intense localness of these relics may account for the remarkable perseverance of his memory in these parts – so it is all the sadder that nothing of his shrine remains, and there is no mention of any shrine here in the few surviving records of the mediæval church.

It is unlikely to have survived the Reformation, and if it did, it will have been destroyed during the Civil War – smashed, looted in the 1540s or the 1640s. A ghost remains: immediately above the apex of the south door in the porch is the niche where his image stood, watching over his parishioners as they conducted their business in the porch and entered and left the church itself.

The shrine was quite possibly sited in the north transept (the Dairy), as many patronal saints were, and its desecration may explain the subsequent use of that space over several centuries for very unecclesiastical purposes (see p. 9).

The Anglo-Saxon and Norman Church

There was a Norman church where the church now stands, and there was very likely an Anglo-Saxon building here before that – and, depending upon when the move in from the cliffs took place, there may have been a Celtic church before that. The Guide section of this book traces what is known (and half-known and guessed) about the development of the church fabric and represents pretty much all that can be said specifically about the building for that period. However, the closeness of the history of St Levan to that of St Buryan, and many clues and trends in regional and national life, enable us to flesh out more of the story.

The Anglo-Saxons invaded Britain almost as soon as the Romans left, but Cornwall did not become fully part of their kingdom until 936. The chief effect of the Saxon presence in Britain before this may have been to emphasize Cornwall's isolation, first from Wessex and places east, then from Wales and finally from Devon. Cornish culture did become distinctive in this period: it was more literate than Anglo-Saxon culture was, and it had some (rapidly deteriorating) Latin; and most importantly, it was Christian and it was Celtic.

It would be nice to date the coming of Anglo-Saxon power to St Levan fairly precisely to about 931, when Æthelstan, grandson of King Alfred, is supposed to have defeated the Cornish king Howell at Boleit (said by some to be Boleigh in St Buryan,[32]) but this story was invented later. There may have been a battle at Boleigh, but Hywel was king of south-west Wales not Cornwall, and there is no contemporary record of Aethelstan being in Cornwall at all. St Buryan did have an ancient Charter, and from very early it was said to have been granted by Æthelstan. However, very few charters claiming to be granted by Æthelstan have been accepted as completely genuine: many of them are inaccurate, or deliberately altered, copies; others still are unqualified frauds.[33] All we now have of the St Buryan Charter is a copy made by Bishop Grandisson of Exeter in 1352 of a copy made in 1238 by Bishop Brewer – a copy, or a forgery, or a bit of both.

It has been suspected of being forged not least because of egregious mistakes in its wording: for example it has the date as "5 October 943 in the 6th year of his reign" – when Æthelstan was dead by then, his sixth year as king being 930. On the other hand, a forger would surely have been more careful over something as checkable (even in 1238) as a date; perhaps it was a slip of the pen. And why didn't a forger working for a 13th-century Bishop of Exeter – or Duke of Cornwall – produce a document more useful to his master, perhaps defining rights and privileges more clearly?

Whoever wrote the Æthelstan Charter, it became very contentious when the Crown and the Bishop came to dispute each other's authority in the 14th century (see below). Some recent scholarship has looked on it with kindlier eyes,[34] and it seems safe to treat it as based on a genuine original (i.e., granted by proper authority, although not necessarily Æthelstan's). At some point before the Conquest, or at least before the Domesday Book, a grant of this sort was made: no one ever disputed its terms, and all that was (eventually) controversial was the meaning of one word in it: "free."

The Charter records that Æthelstan gave some of the land he owned "in the place called the Church of St Buryan." Most of the places named are traceable as still-existing farms and hamlets; one was quite likely in St Levan – 'Treikyn' was surely 'Trethyn', today known as Treen, the largest settlement in the parish. One of the prebendaries of the collegiate church at St Buryan was 'of Trethyn,' and it seems reasonable to suppose that this was because the church held land there.

The granting of a Charter at this date means that St Buryan (which means St Levan too) had accepted the Roman rite,[35] and this meant, above all, submitting to the authority of the archbishop of Canterbury. There was also a change in religious practice. What little evidence there is of Cornish forms shows how varied practice was. Throughout western Christendom in the early middle ages, a bishop could do little to ensure conformity; the Pope had even less power. Thus even if we knew what went on in St Just, say (which we do not), Divine Service at St Levan might have been rather different. Perhaps Celtic Christianity at this time was not as different from Roman Catholic Christianity as has been thought, simply because neither grouping was monolithic enough for such comparisons to be made – and because, unlike some other dissident communities, the Celtic Christians never disputed the authority of the Pope.[36]

There was however at least one important and less disputed difference between the Celtic and the Anglo-Saxon churches: their organization. The Celtic system was based on communities, typically gathered around a holy man – such as Selevan may have been – and persisting after his death through devotion to his relics and teaching; the Anglo-Saxon system was part of the continental Roman system and, while also venerating its saints, was hierarchical, with archbishops and bishops with dioceses with defined boundaries. Roman Christianity brought a highly structured and bureaucratic system of parishes: enumerated, tithed and taxed.

A dependent chapel

Domesday says that there was a collegiate church in St Buryan ('Eglosberrie') in 1066, staffed by a community of canons. Perhaps then – perhaps as early as the Charter, certainly by the early 1200s – St Levan was a dependent chapel of St Buryan, and it stayed so until 1864. For example, in 1313, Bishop Stapledon wrote "[to] the church of St Buryan…, and the Chapels dependent on the same."[37] From about 1300, when in effect the Crown seized the Deanery, until the death of the last Dean over 550 years later, the parishioners of St Buryan, St Levan and Sennen never had the services of more than a curate or two, and sometimes not even that. Moreover, during this period, because the Bishop had no jurisdiction, and the Deans were poor record-keepers, there are virtually none of the usual documents to consult: no terriers, for example (property lists).[38] This is why so little is known directly of the history of St Levan: but a surprising amount can be learnt from the traces which have survived.[39]

St Levan is not mentioned in the Domesday Book, but then neither are many other places in west Cornwall which are known to have existed at that time. It was probably already subject to St Buryan, because of the strong similarities between the arrangements at St Buryan in 1086 and 1214, by which latter time St Levan was definitely involved. In much of what follows, for 'St Buryan' read also 'St Levan.'

At the time the Domesday clerks came through, St Buryan was owned by Count Robert of Mortain, William the Conqueror's half-brother. He had helped himself to about three-quarters of the land belonging to the minster – it had been worth 40s a year when Robert received it (in about 1072) but by 1086 was worth only 10s – but he and his heirs left sufficient with the church to support a small community of canons. According to Domesday, the canons had one hide of land – an imprecise measure, it meant enough land to support a peasant family, usually about 120 acres. Importantly, it was noted that the land was 'free,' but unfortunately it did not say what 'free' meant, an omission which came to cause such trouble.

The Royal Peculiar
The Crown versus the Bishops

There is nothing in the record about St Buryan or St Levan for over a hundred years after 1086. Robert of Mortain probably made himself patron of the church, with the right to appoint the Dean, and when the possessions of Robert's son William were confiscated in 1106, Henry I may have seized this right. However it came about, by 1214 St Buryan (and St Levan) belonged to the Crown – to King John. By 1259, the advowson of St Buryan belonged to John's younger son Richard earl of Cornwall. This meant Richard could nominate the Dean, but he had no share of its revenues or rights. The advowson "remained in the hands of the earls and dukes of Cornwall until the Reformation, except when the earldom or duchy was vacant, in which case it passed to the crown."[40]

The income of the dean and canons came chiefly from the rental of the church's land and the tithes of the parish. The tithes were worth more than the land: Sennen had joined St Levan as part of St Buryan parish, making it large by any standards (about 11,500 acres in total). The Dean seems to have been lord of the largest piece of church-owned land, that around the church, and he also received most of the tithes. In 1291 a papal taxation valued the Dean's share at £20 per annum: well over three times that of the other canons put together.[41] The Dean had other income too: in 1480 his privileges included (and very likely always had included) "religious offerings, fines, escheats, wreck, flotsam, and jetsam,"[42] although there is no estimate of how much this amounted to.

It might be helpful to put these figures in the context of a general taxation of 1336, when St Buryan, at £8. 0s. 2d, paid more taxes than anywhere else in Penwith (twice as much as Madron, for example): indeed only Truro and Bodmin paid more in all Cornwall. St Silvanus (St Levan) parish paid 49s. 5d, only very slightly less than Launceston.[43]

The other canons, three in all, each held a prebend (a stipend), based on the church lands and tithes left over from the Dean's share. The two most valuable seem to have been named after the land which provided their main income: the best was called Rospannel (between Rissick and Bosanketh in St Buryan) and was worth £2 10s 0d in 1291; the next most valuable was then called Trethyn (now Treen in St Levan), and was worth £2 6s 8d. The third 'small' prebend – lands unknown – brought in 15s 0d. In 1548 Rospannel and Trethyn each possessed a messuage (i.e., a dwelling-house and outbuildings) and six acres of land, and the Small Prebend a single acre.

In return for his substantial income, the Dean had various responsibilities. For example, together with the other canons, he was expected to say daily services in the church, or to arrange for a deputy to do so. He was also responsible for the cure of souls throughout the parish, and for providing chaplains to serve the chapels at St Levan and Sennen. All the extant records throughout the life of the Deanery show Sennen and St Levan being served jointly by a chaplain or curate (if at all).

The Dean was thus an important person in the life of St Levan – even though there is no reason to suppose that any Dean ever set foot in St Levan or its church. He received the tithes and he appointed the curate. The curate in the early years was perhaps the only person in the community who could read or write. From the point of view of the people who had the gift of the Deanery, however, its importance was purely financial. From at

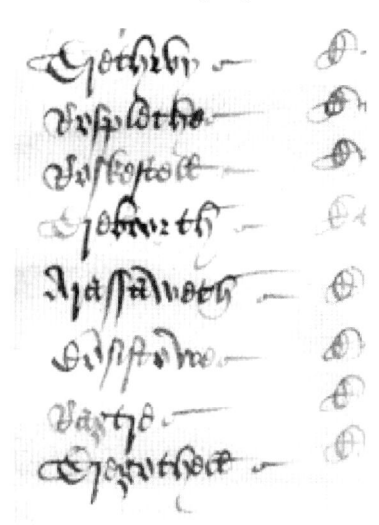

St Levan parish in about 1450: This portion of the Deanery tithe list is one of the few glimpses of St Levan in those days. Reading (with difficulty!) from the top of the extract, we have Trethiby (now Trethewy?), Rospletha, Roskestall, Trefneth?, Arassaweth (now Arden-Sawah), Bosistowe, Raftre, and Tregothall. Apart from Trefneth, which may be a misreading, and Trethiby, which may well be Trethewey, all these farming hamlets still exist. This document is online at www.kings.cam.ac.uk/library/archives/college/hlfproject/counties/cornwall.html. Once you get the hang of the handwriting, it is a fascinating resource. *With kind acknowledgements to King's College Library, Cambridge (KCAR/6/2/136/2 SBU/3 Page One).*

least the early 13th century, and probably before, it was used to support men at court, often King's Clerks – in other words, senior civil servants, who never came here and who may have had only the vaguest idea of where it was. (Appendix A lists the Deans whose names have survived.)

For a few brief years in the middle of the 15th century, the Deanery was owned by King's College Cambridge – which did keep records, some of which survive, including tithe lists[44] – a unique glimpse of the involvement of the people of St Levan with their church. Most if not all the holdings in the district appear on them, including the farming hamlets of St Levan.

The livings associated with St Levan Church were in the gift of the Crown or the earls of Cornwall, but throughout the 13th century the Deanery was subject to the authority of the bishops of Exeter in the normal way. For example, and crucially, Bishop Brewer (of Exeter) visited St Buryan on 26 August 1238 to dedicate the church, presumably after a rebuilding. Bishop Brewer granted an indulgence of thirty days to those who visited St Buryan at the anniversary of the dedication (which must have been popular with St Levan folk, as it involved a walk of only three or four miles), and he ratified the charter said to have been granted by Æthelstan when he founded or endowed St Buryan, including its 'free' status and its right of (very extensive) sanctuary.

In 1300 Earl Edmund died without an heir, and the gift of the Deanery reverted to the crown. The King (Edward I) then claimed St Buryan as a royal free chapel (aka a Royal Peculiar), the effect of which was to remove from the bishops of Exeter all power over the Deanery. Within a couple of years, the King made one of his clerks, Ralph of Manton, Dean.

Bishop Grandisson, like Bishops Bitton and Stapledon before him, strongly opposed the idea that St Buryan was a royal free chapel, and were unhappy with the Deanery being *sine cura* (a benefice without cure [care] of souls – i.e., a sinecure). The evidence was not all their way, however. In part it depended on what had been meant by 'free' – the word used in Domesday and in the Æthelstan Charter. Grandisson argued that 'free' referred to the special sanctuary at St Buryan; the Crown and its adherents interpreted it to mean 'free of episcopal jurisdiction,' and could point to Deans having been appointed by the Crown before Edward's time without any great protests from Exeter. ('Free' actually meant 'free of tax.') As for episcopal protests at the Deanery being a sinecure, Bishop John Kirkby of Ely had been Dean in the 1270s and 80s without complaint from Exeter.

The case dragged through the courts for 50 years and is the only reason that we know anything at all about St Levan at this juncture. For example, from 1310 Bishop Stapledon refused to supply chrism to the Deanery. (Chrism is holy oil, blessed by a bishop for use, amongst other things, in baptism and confirmation, and for the consecration of communion vessels.) This meant that no one in St Buryan, St Levan and Sennen was being offered Communion, or being baptised or confirmed; it is not clear how long this state of affairs persisted, but it must have caused great distress to the innocent parishioners. Worse was to come.

In 1328, the King commanded the new Bishop, John Grandisson, to "abstain" from exercising Ordinary Jurisdiction in St Buryan (a bishop is an 'ordinary').[45] There is no record of a reply from the Bishop, and a few months later there was a very unseemly fight in St Buryan churchyard between the Dean (John de Maunte, the King's man) and Richard Beaupré (the prebendary of Trethyn, an appointee of the previous bishop and from a Norman-Cornish family), and their respective supporters. The most remarkable aspect of the matter must be that not only a prebendary, but *the Dean himself* was here! It is the only certain instance of a Dean of St Buryan being sighted in the Land's End peninsula until the 18th century.

The Dean wanted Beaupré out, and some at least of the local people were on the Dean's side. In the event, the Dean and forty-three others were arrested by the Bishop's men, and Grandisson suspended the sacraments in the Deanery and threatened to excommunicate anyone who continued to resist his authority. Resistance did continue, however, because that November Grandisson came as far as St Michael's Mount, where he excommunicated three people by name, and all who impeded the bishop's jurisdiction. Terrified by the risk of excommunication, 18 people submitted to the bishop and were absolved by him, but the dispute did not end. A year later, according to the Bishop, his men would not go to the Deanery "for fear of death or mutilation."[46]

At one level, this was a game being played at a distance by powerful people who never concentrated long enough on the problem to resolve it, but amused themselves by stirring the pot from time to time and watching the sparks fly; their pride and their purse were involved, but they had more important matters to occupy them. In St Buryan (and St Levan and Sennen) however, it was real. Immortal souls were in peril, their churches were neglected and at times their children went unbaptised and unconfirmed. Whatever they did, they offended either the Bishop or the King. There were also local politics involved: men like Richard of Penrose and Richard Vyvyan, accused and excommunicated by the Bishop in 1328, were undoubtedly large fish in this small pond, who could make life difficult in many little ways – and probably some quite big ways too – for lesser fry who disagreed with them; and moreover they were on the side of the King who, when it came down to it, was a far more frightening enemy than the Bishop.

This particular crisis was resolved in 1336, when Grandisson, despite the risks of venturing so far west, went to St Buryan in person. The Bishop had a strong sense of theatre, and the spectacle he laid on for the Deanery must rank as one of the most impressive ever seen here. He had three knights to guard him, and a large retinue of clergy and servants. On 12th July, presumably in St Buryan Church, Grandisson addressed the 'major parishioners' in French and English, and Henry Marsely, rector of St Just-in-Penwith, rendered his words into Cornish for everyone else. The parishioners' reply demonstrated an intelligent grasp of their situation: they wanted to do nothing which would prejudice the King's rights, but at the same time they wished in future to obey the Bishop and his officers. The 'major parishioners' promised in English and French, the rest in Cornish. Kneeling, everyone sang the ancient hymn "Veni, Creator Spiritus." The bishop condescended to absolve them, and then preached on I Peter ii[25]: "For ye were as sheep going astray; but you are now returned unto the Shepherd and Bishop of your souls," Marsely translating once more into Cornish. [47] Finally, Grandisson "tonsured many clerks from the parish, confirmed 'innumerable' children, and received oaths of obedience from the priests who served the church, of whom there were five."[48] Grandisson also noted the names of the men who signed the statement that day,[49] some of whom were from St Levan: for example Joceus Treboer (likely from Trebehor).

Within a day or two, Prebendary de Maunte attended on Grandisson at his manor-house at Bishop's Clyst (over a hundred miles from here, in Devon). De Maunte was politic enough for the Bishop to remove the excommunication and to allow him access to his rights and revenues, except where they clashed with the Bishop's.[50]

Still, the struggle between Crown and Church continued. As late as 1352, 16 years after Grandisson's performance at St Buryan, the Black Prince (the current owner of the advowson) was complaining that the Bishop (who was still Grandisson) was once more denying chrism to the parishes, and refusing to confirm children or to ordain clergy there. Grandisson's lengthy reply has survived and is the source of much of what is known about the whole dispute — indeed of the whole early history of the Deanery. From this we know that the dispute was still unsettled and that whatever *modus vivendi* had been arrived at in the 1330s, by the 1350s matters were as bad as ever. The Dean, the prebendaries and, according to Grandisson, the parishioners too, had all once more refused to acknowledge his authority.

The papers Grandisson drew together to support his case have been preserved in his Register, and include a copy of what may or may not be Æthelstan's charter.[51] Despite this effort and the merits of his case, this is the last that is heard of the dispute. The reason is probably not far to seek: the Black Death had struck in 1348 and by the beginning of 1350, perhaps a third of the population of Cornwall was dead. The clergy in the diocese, as elsewhere, were disproportionately hit,[52] and the struggle over the Deanery of St Buryan was more or less forgotten. Indeed, Grandisson lived another 17 years, but he never raised the matter again with the Crown or its representatives, and neither did his successors. As Orme puts it:

> St Buryan became a royal free chapel, whose dean was appointed by a mere grant from the king or the duke of Cornwall. Its parish [i.e., including St Levan and Sennen] was reconstituted as a peculiar jurisdiction, in which the dean and his official exercised the powers that normally belonged to the bishop, including the enforcement of Church law and the probate of wills.[53]

If there was little to be known about St Levan up to this date because of its dependence on St Buryan, we now find St Buryan itself almost disappearing from the record. There are odd fragments, mostly giving the names of Deans or prebendaries; otherwise, apart from the King's College documents already mentioned, there is almost nothing from 1352 until the Reformation.

In 1421 Pope Martin V granted a "relaxation for 2 years and 2 quarantines of enjoined penance to Penitents on Easter Monday visiting and giving alms for the repair of the church and the chapel of the Saint in the said parish of St Levan."[54] This was a common way of raising funds for churches in need, and it underlines the neglect which St Levan was continuing to suffer.

About 35 years later, in 1473, the King (now Edward IV) commissioned an enquiry into allegations against the character and activities of the Dean (Robert Knolles) and his colleagues and officers. The commission was soon cancelled, and nothing more was heard of the matter, but given the history of the Deanery, there is every reason to assume that the same old games were being played at the expense of the parishioners.

The Deans continued to be absentees, usually clerks or chaplains to the King or Duke of Cornwall, and with a large number of other benefices: for example, Adam Moleyns (briefly Dean in 1438) was also Bishop of Chichester, and eventually held in addition 14 rectories and 11 prebends – "an outrageous pluralist" indeed, as a contemporary called him, but also an outstanding administrator and a noted humanist scholar.[55]

The End of Mediæval St Levan

Despite the Royal claims, there was a strong connection between St Buryan and Exeter Cathedral from the mid-15th to the early 16th centuries:[56] for example, Dean Stukeley (1439-45) was also archdeacon of Exeter, Dean Ryse (1509-22) was cathedral treasurer. None of these men had much incentive to visit such remote churches, whose revenues they could 'farm' (lease in return for money). When the antiquary John Leland visited Cornwall in 1536, he wrote that the Dean and prebendaries "almost be nether [i.e. none of them] there". ...Not at St Buryan, and certainly not at St Levan either.

Very late in the mediæval records – just before Henry VIII moved against the monasteries – there is some information which shows how the absentee clergy of the Deanery may have managed their responsibilities. The 1535 *Valor Ecclesiasticus* (another tax record) shows 20s. (i.e. £1) paid by the Dean to Robert Vyvian as the steward of his lands: he is presumably of the same family as the Richard Vyvyan who was excommunicated by Bishop Grandisson in 1328, still closely but now more happily involved in church affairs.

Also shown is the Dean paying an annual fee of 13s. 4d. to James Gentill to manage his ecclesiastical jurisdiction. James Gentill was amongst other things provost of Glasney College, Penryn (near Falmouth) and Vicar of St. Uny, Lelant.[57] Most if not all the Deans will have had a similar arrangement because, to take just one example, the Deanery court proved wills and issued letters of administration for those who had died intestate. No other body could do this, and it is hard to see a community surviving long without wills being legally proved.

St Levan may have represented one extreme, where the neglect and abuse cried out for reform; close to the other, perhaps, was Morebath, in Devon. This parish had the benefit of a devoted long-term resident priest, Christopher Trychay, who was vicar from 1519 to 1574 – and his annotated account-book for all but eight of those years survives. In *The Voices of Morebath*, Eamon Duffy uses it to describe not only how the pre-Reformation liturgical life of the church – its daily, weekly and annual round of ritual and worship – involved the parishioners, but also how intricately involved the church was with the government of the parish – caring for the sick, providing alms for the poor, giving some education to children, collecting the King's taxes, promulgating and carrying out central government policies – as well as supporting its priest and keeping the church in good repair.[58]

Duffy's account has been criticized as romantic, but it is also a useful counterweight to the standard story of the late mediæval church, which emphasizes the abuses to a degree which would have gladdened Henry VIII's heart. The parish was the main source of government for the ordinary man and woman, and as such it had to raise money – to maintain the church and its shrines, to help pay the priest, to look after its old and poor. At Morebath and many other places, for example, the young men brewed the 'church ales', which were kept in the church-house and sold to parishioners, especially at feasts and high days; farmers took turns, year on year, to care for church's sheep, and the money from those beasts belonged to the parish; young women saved pennies to keep a light burning in the Lady Chapel. All but the very poorest would leave something to the church at their death — money, cloth, jewellery — and the goods would usually be sold, often to other parishioners, and the cash added to the stores. Men, and women too, took turns to manage the various stores, and were accountable to the priest for them.

This approach suggests that the neglect and worse that St Levan suffered for centuries was far from the whole story. There was probably a church-house at St Levan, and that is where the ales would be sold. We know that there were guilds at St Buryan, for example: in 1454, there were at least four,[59] and if there were none at St Levan, people could have gone to the Buryan groups. The people who lived here had to get by somehow, and getting by in the Middle Ages meant spiritual as well as material succour. If the Dean and the prebendaries were absent, and the curates they sent in their stead unreliable and corrupt (which they cannot all have been), the parishioners were not totally without resources. For most, the church was still the centre of their lives.

Proof of this is in St Levan's church-building record: the stone church of early Norman times, its larger replacement 200 years later, the tower crafted from expensive ashlar in the 15th century, and the last great, abandoned building scheme in the early 16th century — each represented a huge expenditure by this tiny community. The Dean will have had to give permission, and perhaps he sent a few pounds, but on the ground it was at one time perhaps the curate, or another time the Dean's steward, or a pious parishioner with money and time on his hands, who had the vision and made sure it happened, calculating, planning, chivvying and driving forward each project in spite of the corruption of the Deanery. The people of this corner of the world, never rich, usually peripheral, neglected by the people charged with their care, and milched of tithes and taxes which seldom benefited them, nonetheless created and maintained this beautiful church.

The Reformation in St Levan

Reform

The Reformation saw the Crown seizing many of the assets of the Church.

What had begun as a means of effecting the divorce of Henry VIII from Katherine of Aragon very soon became a means of raising revenue for the Crown – chiefly to be spent on unsuccessful wars.

At the end of 1534, Parliament declared that King Henry "shall be taken, accepted and reputed the only supreme head on earth of the Church of England".[60] The Pope's authority was no longer recognized in England, and the Crown had absolute control over the church. There was no tradition of heresy or dissent in these parts, and the impact of these changes, and those which followed, must have left people terrified, when they were not bewildered. In 1531 the ex-priest Thomas Benet had been burned in Exeter for proclaiming the Pope to be the Antichrist; three years later, Hugh Latimer was licensed to preach something not dissimilar in St Mary Major in the same city.

In 1536, most of the traditional holy days were abolished. A Bible in both Latin and English was to be set up in every church (at the church's expense), and the priest was to explain the Ten Articles to his congregation. Shrines and cults were discouraged, though not banned outright (yet). It was from about this time that parish registers of baptisms, marriages and burials were required to be kept.

The dissolution of the monasteries was beginning, but St Buryan escaped – for now – being only a collegiate church. The strategic importance of St Michael's Mount, then a Benedictine house, meant that the buildings at least were maintained, and survive today, but the monks were sent away, and soldiers set in their place: a crude and obvious difference. St Levan will also have noticed when James Gentle (the 'local' representative of the Dean of St Buryan) lost his position as provost of Glasney so that Thomas Cromwell could oblige a political ally.[61]

In 1538, a new set of Royal Injunctions was issued, the most radical of which were against images, cults, pilgrimages, rosaries, candles and other "superstitions." Everywhere, the lights before the various shrines were put out; precious items presented to the shrines were sold. Funds still had to be raised, but their purpose was altered, away from the gilding of images and the keeping of candles, and towards the care of the poor of the parish, and paying increased taxes.

In July of the first year of Edward's reign (1547), even more radical Injunctions were promulgated, and profoundly changed the look of the parish church. Statues and shrines were to be destroyed, and crucifixes and stained glass removed; banners and processions were no longer tolerated, and candles were allowed only at the high altar. This is probably when St Levan lost its statues of Selevan, and his shrine; and its stained glass was smashed. The brewing and sale of church ales were also prohibited, in the interest of public order, it was said, but certainly at great loss to church funds. At the same time, the church was expected to raise the same amount of money. This brought many parishes to the verge of bankruptcy, St Levan perhaps among them.

One thing that is known of St Levan at about this time (i.e., 1535-50) is that, as in many places throughout the land, the rebuilding of the church stopped. The south aisle had already been completed, but the north aisle was never built. There were two reasons for this halt: first, the aisles had been needed so that the parishioners could process around the church (for example at Corpus Christi), and such processions were now banned. Secondly, what

Benefice	Beneficiary in 1536	Valor (1536)	Chantries (1548)	The money coming from:
Dean	Thomas Bagh	£ 9 15s. 11d	£ 9 14s. 1½d	Land and from court fees
Rector	"	£48 12s. 0d	£54 1s. 0d	Great and small tithes
Prebendary of Rospannel	John Wescott	£ 7 7s. 8d	£ 7 6s. 8d	Endowment of land, and some tithes
Prebendary of Trethyn	John Byase	£ 7 0s. 0d	£ 6 19s. 4d	Endowment of land, and some tithes
Small prebendary	John Longe	£ 2 0s. 0d	£ 2 4s. 0d	Endowment of land, and some tithes
Chantry priest	Benedict Phellype	£ 5 10s. 0d	£ 5 0s. 0d	?
TOTAL		£ 80 4s. 7d	£ 80 5s. 1½d	

Annual income of the Deanery of St Buryan in the *Valor Ecclesiasticus*, 1535 and Chantry Certificates 1548[64]

money there was in St Levan was no longer available for the church-fabric; it was over 300 years before there would be sufficient funds for more than urgent patching-up, and even then it was touch-and-go. The positioning of the arch across the transept into the 'Dairy' indicates what had been intended, a reminder of how total the collapse of the old order was.

On top of all this, prayers for the dead were no longer approved of, and so the chantries were to be suppressed, and their goods seized for the Crown. St Buryan had a chantry, where priests were paid to say masses for the soul of Æthelstan and others; it disappeared. But – perhaps because the Crown already owned it – the church itself survived.

Information about these depredations, and about the parishes, has survived in two contemporary sources.[62] Here we find a well-nigh unique statistic about the Deanery, its population: about 1,050 people were housselled (i.e., received communion) in the church of St Buryan, and 400 each in each of the two chapels of St Levan and Sennen. Two years later the figures were much the same, suggesting a total population, including children, of between 2,200 and 2,700, and a population for St Levan of between 500 and 600.[63]

The previous table puts together some of the other information from the *Valor* and the Chantry Certificates. The small differences between these two accounts may be explained by changes in land-values: either way, the Deanery of St Buryan was a valuable property. It is also likely that its lands were the same in 1548 as they had been in 1086 in Domesday – and the same too as in Æthelstan's charter.

All that was about to end. The chantry was suppressed and the Crown (by now the young Edward VI) seized the lands: in 1549 much of it was sold to Sir Thomas Pomeroy of Berry Pomeroy, in Devon. In the 17th century, the manor of Buryan was amongst the thousands of acres owned by the Buller family in Devon and Cornwall, and in the early 20th century these lands were described as "the nucleus of the manor of St Buryan" and as belonging to Robert Tonkin Esq.[65] This does not seem to have included any land in St Levan.

Also sold in 1549 were the right to present to the Deanery (i.e., to put forward candidates as Dean) and the advowson (i.e., the right to appoint to the position). The existing senior clergy were pensioned off, and the commissioners recommended that three vicarages be endowed for each of the Deanery parishes – St Buryan, St Levan and Sennen – with stipends of £20 at St Buryan and £10 each at the other two. In the meantime the existing chaplains were ordered to remain in office with wages of £8 at the mother church and £6 10s. 0d. at each of the two chapels. This was presumably paid for by the tithes, which were not sold off.

This "meantime" lasted in effect for more than 300 years. The Deanery's income fell somewhat, but its duties, and therefore the costs of paying others to carry them out, decreased by more: St Buryan was no longer a collegiate church: the prebendaries and the chantry were gone. At St Levan, one can imagine pleasure, perhaps even jubilation, at the news that the Deanery was going and that they were to have their own vicar. How long did that mood last, and when did people realize that amidst all the changes which they had not sought, the one thing they very probably *did* want was not going to be?

The Prayer Book Rebellion

Perhaps disillusionment came as soon as the Cornish leaders of the Prayer Book Rebellion were executed.

In January 1549, the Act of Uniformity ushered in the Book of Common Prayer. This was a wholly revised liturgy, in English, and was to replace the Mass from Whit Sunday, which that year fell on 9th June. The rebels disliked the Prayer Book: "…and so we Cornishmen, whereof certain of us understand no English, utterly refuse this new English."[66] Protector Somerset's response was that there were very few towns in Cornwall "but ye shall find more in them that understand English than that understand Latin."[67] This may have been true, but rather missed the point: they may not have known much Latin in St Levan, but they certainly spoke Cornish.

As the rebellion took shape, several local gentry families sought refuge at the Mount, but it fell so quickly, and without loss of life to the rebels, that there are doubts about how loyal these gentry were to the Crown's cause.[68] The rest of the campaign was not so easy for the rebels. The Penwith detachment seems to have moved up to join the thousands camped at Bodmin, who then, at the end of June, joined the Devon men at the siege of Exeter. At one point the rebels had the upper hand, but the tide turned when foreign mercenaries arrived to assist the government forces, and a hideous slaughter ensued. If anyone from St Levan was involved, which is likely, it is unlikely that they made it home.

One man who did not come back and who had a connexion with St Levan was William Alsa. Alsa is a St Buryan name, referring to a hamlet in the west of the parish (now called Alsia). His connexion with St Levan is closer than this, however: on a tax-list of 1524, we find him described as a chaplain (*capellanus*), and resident in St Levan. A hundred years ago, one local historian thought that "[Alsa] was probably a resident priest serving St Levan and perhaps St Sennen under the Dean of St Burian."[69] If this is so, then William Alsa is the first priest of St Levan known to us. Prof Orme however is not convinced, and thinks that Alsa was more likely an independent priest in the Deanery.[70] By 1536, he was certainly vicar of Gulval (just the other side of Penzance), where the Alsa family[71] held land. In 1549, he was hanged for his part in the Rebellion.

Thus passed the Commotion, also known as the Camping Time, because of the camps which the rebels had set up.[72] The memory of the horror of the massacre and of the desolation of the defeat lasted long in Cornwall, and in Devon too.

The Elizabethan Settlement

The Deanery fades from view, and St Levan with it, for nearly 30 years. Thomas Bagh, the last Dean of the collegiate church, took his pension and went we know not where; nor do we know who his successor was. This may be when the painted walls of St Levan church were first whitewashed; it was when the Ten Commandments and the Lord's Prayer in English were displayed in the church. A later copy of the former can still be seen let into the floor of the Lady Chapel; then, like the copy of the Lord's Prayer is still, they would have been on the walls.

The failure of the Prayer Book Rebellion meant that Protestantism prevailed – not because that Prayer Book was especially Protestant (it was not), but because there was no one left willing to oppose the more radical measures which followed. Altars were removed, and instead communion-tables were placed further up the chancel, or even in the nave.[73]

The (very Protestant) Second Book of Common Prayer was published at the end of 1552. Cornwall, three and a half years after the disaster of its Rebellion against the first book, accepted it. And then Edward died. After a brief attempt to secure Lady Jane Grey the throne, Edward's sister Mary succeeded to popular acclaim – probably loudly echoed in St Levan. The old religion was going to be restored. The new Bishop at Exeter, Miles Coverdale, was allowed to slip away abroad and the ancient Bishop Veysey was reinstalled. The altars were put back (or made anew), noses were remodelled on statues, and the Mass was restored.

And then Mary married Philip of Spain. It was an extremely unpopular alliance. It was this – and perhaps Philip's embargo on the English engaging in the African trade in which several Cornishmen were very interested – which destroyed most Cornish support for Catholicism.[74] It is the last we hear of Cornish opposition to the government for nearly 100 years.

In November 1558, Mary died childless, and her sister Elizabeth became Queen. No one can have known that this was the last swing of the Reformation pendulum, that (ignoring the Civil War) Elizabeth's religious compromise would remain more or less untouched until today. What St Levan made of it we do not know.

It is 1578 before a Dean of St Buryan appears in the record again: William Fairchild. A 1592 lawsuit involving Fairchild and others at St Buryan suggests that there was still confusion about the status of all three parishes: "Whether the church there is the parish church, or is called the King's Free Chapel, College, or Collegiate Church of St Burian?"[75] The decision must have been that St Buryan was not a parish church, because the Deanery was restored to virtually what it had been before the Reformation (minus its lands). The curates were surely still doing the work, however, as anonymous to the historical record as ever.

The 17th Century
A named curate for St Levan

Despite the Chantry Commissioners' plan to create three ordinary parishes out of the Deanery of St Buryan, it remained intact – as intact, that is, as they had left it: the land had gone, and the chantry, and probably a great deal of plate and relicts; the staff had collapsed from as many as six priests, not counting absentees, to three: an (absent) Dean and two curates – one for St Buryan and one for St Levan and Sennen together. There was still no rectory anywhere in the Deanery.

By 1637 at the latest, the old methods of the sinecure were back in place (if they ever went away): Walter Ralegh (a nephew of the famous Sir Walter) became Dean. In the old manner, Ralegh was a pluralist who probably never came here, but there was an important difference: he was a full-time practicing clergyman, not a civil servant. This remained the pattern until the Deanery itself was finally abolished: with the exception of the last Dean, it remained in the hands of practising, if absentee, clergy. Moreover, the invisibility of the men who did the work was beginning to change: we know who Ralegh's curate was.

Symon William's name appears in the 1642 Protestation Return for St Levan, as the curate.[76] The Revd Symon is the first clergyman whose name we can attach to St Levan with complete confidence: we *know* that he lived and worked in the parish of St Levan, and held services in the church. He signed the Return, being of course literate: as such he was in a small minority in the parish – only nine other men wrote their names, and probably some of them could write little else. Neither of the St Levan constables could write, and only one each of the two churchwardens and two overseers.

Further evidence of the curate's literacy is in the will and testament of his colleague Richard Tapper at Buryan. Tapper died in 1643, and Symon William was executor. In the inventory of his worldly worth is: "More his Library of bookes valued by ye Ministere of Sunning [Sennen] and St Levan att the some of £13 – 06s – 8d."[77] Tapper's library was worth almost as much as everything else he owned, and Symon William was capable of valuing it. There was a Dean in office for at least another three years before he was ejected, and it is very likely that Symon William was ejected too.[78]

Civil War

The impact of the Civil War on Cornwall was immense, and St Levan did not escape. The gentry of the county were divided, but the generality of the people, guided perhaps by their clergy, were Royalist, and Cornwall was a staunch if isolated Royalist stronghold for much of the war. A hundred years before, they had fought and died for the old religion; now they would fight and die for the King, even if they did not like him, or his taxes, very much.[79]

It was in recognition of this effort that the King wrote a letter of thanks to the people of Cornwall from "his camp at Sudeley Castle, the 10th September, 1643," which in many parishes was painted on a large board and hung in the church: the King Charles Boards still hang in many Cornish churches, and St Levan's hung in the church for over 200 years. (For what then happened to it, read on!)

In early 1645, Cornwall seemed safe for the Royalists; but Fairfax and Cromwell were beginning their march westward. By now the 15-year-old Prince of Wales (who was also of course the Duke of Cornwall) was titular head of his father's western army; he and his exhausted troops were forced back into Cornwall. As things went from bad to worse, Prince Charles escaped from Pendennis Castle (at Falmouth) to France via the Scilly Isles and Jersey. There is a story that he stopped at several places *en route*, before finally embarking from Sennen Cove. He may therefore have passed through St Levan – indeed, if he did go by land for the last stage to Land's End, it would have been hard for him to avoid doing so; but we have no proof of this. With the Prince out of the country, the Royalists surrendered Cornwall: in April 1645, the Mount capitulated and in August, Pendennis. It was the end of the First Civil War in Cornwall.

The Second Civil War (1648) happened for the most part far away from Cornwall and St Levan; but there were sympathetic uprisings in the Mount's Bay area and around Helston. People were desperate after years of war, plague and food shortages. Captain James Tresilian of St Levan was an officer of a group of about 200 rebels who took up positions between Penzance and Gulval "sweetly animated by greater men:"[80] evidently Tresilian and Co were in touch with these 'greater men' further up-country, as part of the overall plot. Tresilian will not have been the only St Levan man there, causing great anxiety to the Parliamentarian John St Aubyn, who was now in command of the Mount, and who was faced with the rebels plundering Penzance.

On Monday, 22 May, about one o'clock, they [the Parliamentarians] attacked the rebels in Penzance and seized the town with a loss of only 2 killed and 4 or 5 wounded, while the enemy, according to John Moyle's account, lost 60 or 70 slain, 60 taken prisoner and others drowned.

There is no word here of what became of the St Levan contingent. Overall, the odds do not look good, but Tresilian survived – he was one the three Tresilians of St Levan who were each fined £3.6.8d for their Royalist activities in 1650.[81]

In January 1649 the King was executed:

The elements themselves seemed to play a part in the tragedy. On the same day a great storm broke over west Cornwall; a ship carrying the King's belongings to France was wrecked on Godrevy Island with the loss of all on board, and rocks were overthrown at the Land's End.[82]

One can imagine what they made of that at St Levan.

Much of what remained of the mediæval glory of Cornwall's (and England's) churches after the depredations of the Reformation was now destroyed. The rood screen at St Ives came down at this time,[83] and perhaps that was when the St Levan screen did too. But, as at St Buryan, it was not entirely destroyed.

Joseph Hull

The Parliamentarians seem to have abolished the Deanery, as well as ejecting at least one Dean, Robert Creighton, but the record is then rather confused. At some point there were visiting preachers, but by 1656 at the latest, there was a permanent appointment: that of Joseph Hull, "Rector of St Buryan".[84]

St Levan will not have seen anything like Joseph Hull before, although his life started conventionally enough: born at Crewkerne in Somerset in 1595, and educated at Oxford University, he eventually became Rector of Northleigh, in Devon. As his subsequent career shows, he was a disputatious man, and in about 1632, he resigned from this living and returned to

Crewkerne. His wife Joanna died at about this time.

At Crewkerne, he eventually gathered around him a party of 106 people, and in 1635 they left from Weymouth for the American colonies. They arrived in Boston six weeks later, and then settled nearby; then in 1639 Hull fell out with Governor Winthrop of the Massachusetts Bay colony, and moved to Cape Cod to become a founder of Barnstaple town. Within the year he was on the move again: he went to Maine, and seems to have been content for a decade or more, as an Episcopalian minister.[85] (Episcopalians are, broadly speaking, American Anglicans.) For Hull was not a Congregationalist as most of the New England settlers were; he was an "Episcopalian with moderate Puritan views" – which makes one wonder why he emigrated in the first place.

In 1653, however, the Congregationalists became powerful in Maine, and Hull felt the need to move again. This time, with Cromwell supreme in England, he returned home (his 14 children remained in America, but his second wife, Agnes, came with him). He was Rector of Launceston for a few years before moving to St Buryan, where he arrived in or before 1656.

He features eight times in the annals of the local Quakers, insisting on his tithes despite their religious objections to paying them. We also learn to whom he farmed out his tithes, just like a Dean of St Buryan: in 1658 it was the St Levan man Pascoe Tresilian, presumably a relative of James, the local rebel leader of the Second Civil war. Pascoe had been fined for his Royalist activities not long before, but life presumably had to go on, and now he was working with the system:

> The 23^d day of ye 8th mo: 1658 John Ellis was served with a speciall warrant at ye suit of Pascoe Tresilian whoe farmed ye tithe of Joseph Hull preist of Sennen …[86]

Hull was by no means alone in resisting the claims of the Quakers – there can have been hardly a minister in the land who would not have done the same – but in his case, it seems something more. See another mention of him in these annals:

James Myers: For speaking to preist Hull parson of Burrion att ye lands end hadde beene beaten by ye preist butt that his wiffe helde him.[87]

Hull's wife (Agnes) evidently restrained her husband. However it was not this kind of behaviour which brought Hull's tenure of St Buryan (and St Levan and Sennen) to an end, but the Restoration of the monarchy in 1660 and the subsequent Act of Conformity. This Act required all ministers to subscribe to the Book of Common Prayer; for some reason (but somehow we are not surprised), Hull felt unable to do this, and so became part of the Great Ejection, one of nearly 2,000 ministers who resigned. Poor Joseph Hull was too Episcopalian for Massachusetts and too Puritan for King Charles II.

And so in 1662 he went back to the colonies – to New Hampshire, where he spent most of the remaining three years of his life. He died, aged 70, on one of the Isles of Shoals, off the coast of Maine. The Revd CB Crofts called Hull a "bitter and rabid Puritan,"[88] but Mr. Crofts did not know of Hull's experience on the other side of the Pond. Joseph lacked the gift for contentment. But what, one wonders, did he tell St Levan of the New World? And what did he tell Massachusetts, New Hampshire and Maine of St Levan?

The Latter Days of the Deanery
The Bishops of Exeter

Robert Creighton, the Dean of St Buryan ejected in the 1640s, petitioned the Crown for resumption of the tithes in June 1660, but we know that Joseph Hull did not resign his living at St Buryan until 1662.[89] Perhaps he acted as the Dean's representative for those two years. Those were certainly confused and confusing times.

Seth Ward became Bishop of Exeter in 1663, and for the next 53 years – until 1716 – the Bishop of Exeter was also Dean of St Buryan.[90] The irony of the Crown granting the Bishop what they had fought so fiercely for 300 years earlier may have been lost on contemporaries. Perhaps their concerns were more with maintaining peace and stability than with tracing ancient disputes; or perhaps they laughed until they cried at the inn in Treen.

There was some continuity: Dean Thomas Lamplugh leased "the tithes of S. Burian, March 30, 1683, to Hugh Jones, Esq., of Penrose, and Francis Paynter, gent., of Boskenna, for three years."[91] Hugh Jones had been a tithe farmer of Joseph Hull's in 1661.

Perhaps the most famous Dean of St Buryan was Sir John Trelawney (as Bishop of Exeter 1688-1707): this is the Trelawney of "And Shall Trelawney Die?", a much later poem and song which has become the unofficial Cornish anthem. Sir John never came to St Buryan, let alone St Levan, but at least we know the names of his curates here: William Polkinghorn went on to be Vicar of St Ives in 1705, and John Trenhaile, from Madron, became Rector of Gerrans, in about 1714. He married thrice, each time to a woman named Jane[92]. Little else is known of him.

The Deanery Court

Bishop Seth Ward, the first to combine that post with the Deanery (1662-67), had been an extremely able administrator (as well as a mathematician and astronomer of international repute: he was a founder-member of the Royal Society).[93] Perhaps he instituted the processes by which the Deanery was run for the remainder of its existence. Certainly before the end of the century, procedures were being followed and records were being kept, not just the (incomplete) parish registers, but also the records of the Deanery Court: a collection of drafts, minutes, notes, accounts and legal documents.

Every diocese and Peculiar had its own court, and each court developed its own processes;[94] few were as odd as the Deanery's. From 1662, it was once more a Royal Peculiar, and still not subject to the authority of the Bishop (when he was being Dean the Bishop was *not* a bishop). This meant that it had to have its own court.

It looks as though the Deanery Court sat when there was sufficient business, as this letter from the "Register" of the Court, William Dinham, to Dean Sykes in 1731 suggests:

> I propose (God willing) with y[r] approbation to hold a Court at the Royall Deanery of S[t] Berian about the middle of the Next Month, w[ch] will be the time & people there desire to have it, and shall Gladly receive y[r] Comands relating thereunto.[95]

The court sat in Buryan Church, but when additional meetings were required, they used the inn over the way (where the Belmont B&B now is, formerly the King's Arms).[96] The Court combined three events of a normal parish: the Vestry Meeting, the Visitation and the Court itself. Instructions were sent out, presumably to the curates, by the Dean's clerk:

> to sumon all the churchwardens within the Deanery to bring their psntments [i.e., presentments – statements of things wrong in the parish] & to return new church-wardens; fees of Visitation; Their Originall Register books of their respective parishes to be viewed and allowed togeather with Coppyes of them fairly [sic] written, All that teach school, practise Physick or midwifery to show their Licences, or to extract Licences. All executors to prove the will of the dead, so the next of Kinne to take letters of Admon [i.e., to do with probate]…[97]

Five years later, the instructions also summon those who preach and chirurgeons (surgeons) to show their licences.[98] The Visitation allowed the Dean, or his representative, to "inspect the manners of his people and clergy;"[99] the inspection of the parish registers was part of this, as was the reminder to curates, from at least 1749, that they had to "shew their respective Titles and Orders"[100] – that is, to prove their right to the priesthood, and their licences to preach.

Hardwick's Marriage Act, which came into effect in 1755,[101] added another task to the list. It was intended to stop clandestine marriages, and to this end, processes very similar to those obtaining today were instituted: the calling of banns, the requirements for special licences, and so on. The surrogate, "who hath Power to grant Licences of Marriage" and who in turn had to pay a bond of £100 (held here by the Dean), had to be sworn in every year.[102] Sometimes the surrogate was from outside the Deanery – for example, from the late 1760s for many years, it was the Vicar of Paul – but this may only have happened when the Deanery curates could not afford the bond: the surrogate was often one of the Deanery curates.

In the "vestry" part of the day, the outgoing lay-officials (the churchwardens, the sidesmen, the constables) would render their accounts, and the new men would be sworn in.

Most interesting however are the workings of the Court itself. For example, until 1858, the Church of England dealt with the probate of wills, and here in St Levan that meant, of course, the Deanery. All wills, and all matters to do with people of any substance who died intestate, passed through the Court. Thus over 100 St Levan wills from between 1605 and 1857, most with inventories attached, are preserved in the Deanery archive.[103] The (perfectly lawful) claims which, until 1858, the Court made on the estate of dead parishioners and their heirs was obviously an important source of income, and also of ill-feeling. The fees and stamps were payable upon probate from the end of the 17th century: they were fixed by Parliament, but collected by the Dean. At the turn of the 18th century: estates worth less than £20 attracted no fee; between £20 and £100, the charge was ten shillings, between £100 and £200 it was £2, between £200 and £300, it was £5, and so on. A sliding scale of fees, depending on the relation of the legatee to the testator, also applied to each legacy.[104]

However, the business of probate was expensive: another scrap in the archives is the expense claim of an officer of the Court for a series of trips upcountry in February 173$^{2}/_{3}$, amounting to £7 – 13s – 6d; another undated bit of paper indents for horses, wine, ale, "ordinaries" (i.e., food, or possibly couriers) and accommodation.[105]

More common than probate business, however, was dereliction in the

William Polkinghorne's handwriting: He was curate of St Levan and Sennen 1693-97. This is the earliest document we have signed by a priest who served at St Levan. It is an endorsement on a document of the Deanery Court ordering an excommunication for non-payment of the church rate, and it reads: **"This was fully executed according to due form July the 23d 1693 by me – Wm Polkinghorn Curate."**

CRO: DSB/C/177. By kind permission of the Cornwall Record Office (author's photograph)

matter of the church rate. The oldest surviving St Levan item in this archive concerns Olliver John, who in 1692 was brought before the Court for failure to pay the rate.[106] The church rate was an important source of revenue for local government, and so this was rather like failing to pay council tax now, but it was also a tax in support of the established church, and so failure to pay was sometimes more accurately *refusal* to pay. Whether Olliver John was poor or a Dissenter – or both – is not known, nor can we decide in the many other such cases which came to the Court.

Continued failure to pay resulted in excommunication: this happened to three Sennen men the following year, and their sentence refers to "the great danger of their soules."[107] That particular case provides us with the signature of the St Levan curate (*above*). People thus cast off from the church often came back in following years to beg formally for forgiveness, because the consequences of not doing so were severe: not only was your immortal soul in peril, but your will might not have effect.

Another frequent cause of presentment at the Court was antenuptial fornication: the fact was presumably detected by the birth-date of a child in wedlock. Several couples were summoned to answer for their misdeeds. For example in 1702 John Nicholls and Rachel his wife were cited, as were John Roberts and his wife.[108] There is no mention of the punishment, but it cannot have been regarded as gravely as fornication or adultery (for which there is no record of punishments either): in 1708, Margaret Harvey was called to account for bastardy, having compounded her sin by "naming no father"[109] and in about 1715 we have "John Roberts Gent for Adultery with Jane Bluett his servt Maide."[110] William Dinham, in the 1731 letter quoted above, continued:

> There are pretty many offenders for bastardy &c that have been sumon'd, and contumacious [i.e., have ignored the summons]; I assume you'l be pleas'd to order such to be psented to Excommunicacion, wch probably may be a Means of Reforming them.[111]

From time to time, accusations of slander or libel were brought before the Court by the aggrieved person. In 1756, as a typical example, Stephen

Bennatts brought a case for libel against one of his neighbours for calling his wife Elizabeth the whore of John Deson.[112]

Of direct impact on the church itself was the accusation of "Perturbation of Seating" (strictly, Perturbation of Seat). The wealthier parishioners paid for the right to a pew in the parish church[113] and, according to ecclesiastical law, anyone "disturbed in his alleged private right" should take action not only against the "stranger so disturbing him in his rights," but also against either the churchwardens or the "ordinary" (here, the Dean) whose responsibility it was to provide adequate accommodation for all.[114] In 1755, there is the presentment: "John Osborn for perturbation of seating in St Levan Church at the Instance of Thomas Roberts Esq."[115] It was important to sort out these disputes, not only because of the threat (or reality) of unseemly behaviour in church, but also because pew-rent (collected twice a year by the churchwardens) was a good source of income – in some cases (perhaps in the Deanery) contributing to the curate's pay.[116]

In 1734 the St Levan curate brought a case against:

> the Churchwardens there for not Railing the Communion Table and suffering the pavement to go out of repair, and for suffering the Boys to place theire Hatts on the Communion Table during Divine Service. Psented by me Corker the Curate.[117]

This is very interesting: because the case is against the churchwardens, we know that the communion table was still in the nave, puritan-style, otherwise the responsibility would have been Corker's.

The parishioners of St Levan were either far more law-abiding, or maybe just better at not getting caught, than their counterparts in Sennen, a parish of much the same population. For example, in 1728, a typical year, of 26 parish-based items brought before the Deanery Court, two involved St Levan people, and 11 Sennen. The remaining 13 were from St Buryan, which was larger than St Levan and Sennen combined. There were numerous years when St Levan presented no business for the Court at all… Some of this imbalance can be traced, in the early years at least, to the existence of the Quaker meeting-house at Sennen, but it does not explain the fact that later in the century, after persecution of Quakers had ceased, St Levan remained comparatively more respectable. Since St Levan paid as much as Sennen towards the Court's costs, this may have contributed to feeling against the Deanery and its institutions.

Mention of costs brings us to the question of who paid how much for the Court. Tidy sums were gathered in from outside the Deanery, usually in connexion with probate, but most came from the parishioners, through a share of the church-rate and of the other charges on services rendered by curate or Dean. St Levan seems to have paid about a quarter, Sennen the same, and St Buryan a half. There is an undated note of fees paid to the Court by the churchwardens of the several parishes: St Levan 6/8d, Sennen 6/8d, and St Buryan 13/4d.

A note of "fees pertaining to pstments" (including St Levan at 8/6, and a total of 16s for St Buryan)[118] tells us that the churchwardens had to use church funds to pay the Court to pursue the presentments they forwarded to it. This not only discouraged frivolous complaints but reflected the fact that the accused's behaviour had a potential cost for the parish. Bastards could well become a charge on the community, for example.

Tithes

Paying tithes was very unpopular everywhere, not just in St Levan. The Church had a right to a tenth (tithe) of the agricultural produce of every parish, and in the Deanery they had always provided the majority of the income, even before the land was sold away in 1548: thus the Dean, like any other incumbent, was keen that everyone who should pay did pay.

Tithes were originally due all in kind (i.e. with a tenth of the titheable 'crop'), although over time, there was a shift to cash payments. The incumbent or his agents generally sold off the goods received, perhaps at a nearby market-town where prices would be better: Penzance in our case.[119] A document from 1717 – "A Particular of the manor of paying Tythes within the Deanery of St Buryan as the same hath Been beyond the memory of man agreed to be Customary payments thereof,"[120] – gives a fascinating glimpse of how payment in kind worked. The first particular in the list, for example, requires that the tithe of "all sorts of Corn" be selected by taking the tenth sheaf "forth of the said mow or stack" in the same order in which they were put in—in order to ensure that the Dean was not landed with the poorer-quality sheaves. Another trick which the Dean's agents had their collective eye on was "that 24 Houres Notice be given to the Deane his farmer or his Bailfe [bailiff] Steward Hayne [hayward?] or Agent of the Tything and Carrying the Corn or of Cutting or Tything the Grasse": the Dean's farmer (i.e. the person who had bought the right to the tithe) wanted his men there to check that there was no cheating.

Each family had to pay 4d (something less than 2p) annually for "rootes and garden," but "in case they sell [the vegetables] to pay A fourth of so much as they sell." For every bullock sold to the butcher, the Dean was due one shilling. There were similar rules governing colts, and kids, and cows and calves.

We can also see when some at least of the produce was collected: the hay was assessed when still standing in "Grass Cocks" although it was not collected until "made dry and fit to be housed"; the lamb tithe was payable "upon St Mark's Day being the 25th Day of Aprile yearly"; wool was collected "in the month of June yearly on A certain Day to be appointed by the owner and A Convenient Notice thereof to be given to the Dean his farmer or Agent."

Wages were titheable too, in theory. This early income tax was however notoriously difficult to collect, and it seems to have been rarely tried, aside from on the profits of milling and fishing.[121] From the early 18th century we have evidence of the Dean trying to enforce these rights:[122] he claimed that the pilchard fishery at Penberth (in St Levan) having "heretofore paid No tyth," should henceforth pay in the same way as the "Millett" (i.e., mullet) tithe was reckoned: a third of the catch was the "Netts part" (i.e. reserved to cover the costs of nets), the tithe being calculated on the remaining two-thirds. A little later, in 1743, Dean Sykes tackled Dr. Borlase, Vicar of Madron, over the latter's claiming tithes on a Madron parishioner's Penberth fishery.[123] This tells us for example that the pilchard fishery was not ancient, but that the catching of mullet was; and that some men came from well outside the parish to fish, and kept their boats at Penberth through the winter. We also learn how important the tithes were. Dean Sykes never came here, but he nonetheless took the trouble to write in very strong terms to a colleague about his right to some pilchards. It was a serious matter.

The payment of tithes was obligatory, and had nothing to do with whether or not one was a practicing member of the church. Moreover, the parishioner had no right of appeal.[124] It was for the Dean to go to court – to the hundred court, which met regularly over in Gwithian Churchtown.[125] In 1757, however, matters were resolved before litigation had gone so far. Nicholas Boscawen, who had become Dean the previous year, evidently thought he could get more money by acquiring his tithes in kind and selling them on his own account. The response of the "Inhabitants, farmers and tillers of land residing within the parishes of St. Levan and Sennen" was to enter into a bonded agreement with Francis Paynter, the Register of the Court. The people of those parishes, said the agreement, had been accustomed to pay cash to the former deans of St. Buryan in lieu of tithes, no tithes being paid in kind except corn, grain, hay, fish, geese, pigs and honey. The undertaking was that, should the present Dean bring any legal action to break any of these customs in order to compel payment in kind, Paynter would assess any payments that were made and keep a record of all the tithes paid to the Dean.

There is no further official mention of this matter, or none that survives, but we do have a very unofficial view of it. One of Francis Paynter's sons, known as Francis the Wit for his satiric verses, lampooned Boscawen at least twice, and one of these squibs commented on this case:

> *Let the priest by o'erreaching,*
> *By canting and preaching,*
> *Endeavour to make his tithes double;*
> *Unassisted by law*
> *All the parson can do,*
> *Is no better by G than a bubble.*[126]

Young Francis was in a good position to know about Boscawen's doings, and from these lines we gather that his father's scheme thwarted the more extreme of the Dean's ambitions.

Resentment at paying tithes increased over the years as the population increasingly turned to Methodism, but possibly even worse was seeing people getting away with *not* paying tithes. For example, there is this piece of paper, in an anonymous, barely literate hand:

> July 25th 1774
> 4 Bots went to sea from penden Cove and the Men one and all able pay no Tyth
> Stephen Wisbeck and partners
> Hugh woolcock and partners
> Richard White and partners
> Williams Warren and partners
> In Thomas Mason Bote[127]

These snippets all help to add to our picture of the relationship between St Levan Church and its parishioners. The Dean's tithe-farmer would be about as popular as a modern tax-inspector, we may imagine, but much more familiar; he or one of his men would be round the parish all year, looking out for his portion of the harvest and perhaps negotiating when payments were behindhand; he would be in church most Sundays. For some, the offering of the tithe would be an never-ending battle of wits with "the Deane his farmer or his Bailfe Steward Hayne or Agent"; for others, those with little enough

John Clode's excuse to the Court: The St Levan curate (1714-30) had mislaid the parish register, and this seems to have been his covering note to the Deanery Court for some substitute record: "I protest – coming away in haste to visit a Sick Person – upon the abode I left the Coppy of the Register behind. Therefore must begg of you to take this for it til next Court – I am your very humble servant Jno Clode"
CRO: DSB/C/196/1 By kind permission of the Cornwall Record Office (author's photograph)

to eat at the best of times, or the simply feckless, it would be something to dread; for many, it was just what happened and perhaps even what it was meant to be – a grateful offering to a church which cared for their souls. For us, it is a vivid example of how the church was once very close indeed to the everyday life of its people – whether they liked it or not!

The Deans of St Buryan and the Curates of St Levan

The last Bishop of Exeter to be Dean of St Buryan was the great preacher and controversialist **Ofspring Blackall**, who held both posts from 1708 until his death eight years later. In 1714, he appointed **John Clode** as curate of St Levan and Sennen.

Clode was a very hands-on curate – his signature appears on most of the churchwardens' presentments of his time, for example, which other curates did not tend to do, and he made an extraordinary comment in the baptismal register of 1730: "the third Christian I ever made since I have been Curate here"[128] – which speaks badly either of St Levan's spiritual state

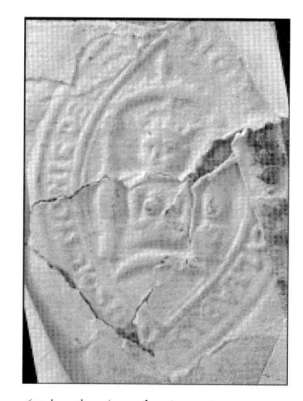

The Deanery Seals: The old seal is lost, and we have only its ghost *(right, above)* – the imprint on a few post-Civil-War documents. There is reason to believe that this was the seal used from a very early date. The new 'burlesque' seal (1717) *(centre, above)* caused something of a scandal (see text). The seal, old and new, would have been in the Deanery perhaps only when the Court was held, or perhaps even only when the Dean was present (in which case, extremely rarely), and likely never in St Levan, but the power it represented, though remote, was very real. The sight of it on the red wax of official documents *(left, above)* will have been familiar to churchwardens and curates alike down the centuries, until 1864 and the end of the Deanery.

CRO: DSB/C/1, DSB/C/197 *By kind permission of the Cornwall Record Office (Author's photograph)*

or Mr. Clode's frame of mind, or possibly both. He was not however always as hands-on as he should have been: there is a note from him to the Register William Dinham (p. 73).[129]

Clode may have been the man behind the "Proposal in Relation to the Fishery," mentioned above (p. 73): his work would have brought him into weekly if not daily contact with the fisheries at Penberth and Sennen Cove (Porthgwarra did not develop until the mid-19th century).

From now on, the Bishops of Exeter were no longer Deans of St Buryan. The next Dean was **John Harris**, Clerk to the Closet of the Princess of Wales. Harris held the post for 23 years, until 1739, and in that time appointed **Robert Corker** and then Jonathan Toup to St Levan and Sennen; he was also Dean when the "Particular" concerning the tithe was drawn up, if not at his instigation, certainly in his interests; but little more is known of him. He was taken to task in the 19th century by local antiquarian Joseph Polsue because he was responsible for "the present oval and ungraceful seal" which "presents a burlesque figure of Athelston."

The new seal (pictured left and centre opposite) was indeed a poor imitation of the previous one (right, the actual impression protected by a tissue cover), which may have been very old indeed. The 'burlesque' seal remained in use until the abolition of the Deanery nearly 150 years later.

Jonathan Toup was appointed curate in 1738 and stayed for 11 years. He was the most distinguished scholar to hold the post, although recognition did not come until much later. He was born in 1713 at St Ives, where his father, also Jonathan, was curate; his mother was Prudence Busvargas of St Just. He was educated at Exeter College, Oxford, graduating in 1736; he came to St Levan and Sennen in 1738, and remained until 1749. As the *Oxford Dictionary of National Biography* puts it, "Toup's tenure of a curacy in a remote village gave him ample leisure to pursue his researches."[130] His first publication, *Emendationes in Suidam* (3 pts, 1760–66), established his reputation amongst fellow textual critics, but his best-known work was an edition of Longinus' *On the Sublime* (1778), which did much to popularize a rather neglected writer. However, although "Toup's scholarship was greatly admired … his critics claimed that his reputation was marred by a churlish, conceited, and supercilious nature." Unfortunately it is not recorded whether he treated his parishioners with similar contempt.

After his mother died in 1773, Toup inherited a considerable property which provided the erstwhile "poor curate" with a large income. At his death 12 years later, he was worth some £12,000: most of his manuscripts went to the Bodleian Library, Oxford. Nothing came to St Levan.

The curate after next was **Richard Pearce** (1754-69), who left a distinct mark on the Deanery: he was, for example, very keen on bells. The treble here at St Levan (1754), and one of the bells formerly hanging at Sennen (1762), were hung in his time: the latter had his name inscribed on it.[131] He had other stakes in the district: "Richard Pearce of St. Levan, Clerk" assigned the lease of two houses in New Street Penzance in 1757,[132] and his name is in the list of subscribers to a 1769 edition of Carew's *Survey of Cornwall*.[133] His feeling for this community shows in the fact that, although he left the Deanery in 1769, he was buried at St Buryan in 1787.

In Pearce's time, Dean Sykes died and was succeeded by **Nicholas Boscawen** (1720-93). The youngest son of the first Viscount Falmouth and Charlotte Godfrey, niece of the Duke of Marlborough, his family was one of the richest in Cornwall. He was Dean of St Buryan from 1756 to 1793. He made history of a sort by actually attending the Deanery Court in 1757, and again in 1782.[134] These are the first recorded instances of the Dean coming to Buryan since John de Maunte was Dean in 1328 – and the only other known instance was 14 years before that, in 1314, when Matthew de Medentor held the post. Boscawen did not however make a good impression:

> . . . a zealous priest
> With Avarice galled the groaning west;
> Rapacious soul he seemed designed
> By nature to oppress mankind:
> His features, maugre all his art,
> Disclosed the baseness of his heart;
> For Satanus took care to place
> A stamp upon his swarthy face. . .[135]

James Bevan was our longest serving curate: from 1775 to 1812. With his wife Elizabeth, he had at least four children, three of whom were baptised at St Levan.[136] His daughter Margaret was buried there in 1791, as was Susanna in 1806. The Revd James was buried here himself in October 1812, and 19 years later his memorial was set up in the Dairy. There is more evidence of how fondly people remembered him. In 1804, he married George Vingoe of Sennen and Elisabeth Hicks (formerly of St. Buryan), at Sennen Church. He also baptised five of their children, and buried two of them. Their seventh child, Margaretta Bevan Vingoe, who arrived seven years after his death, was surely named for him and possibly also for his daughter Margaret.

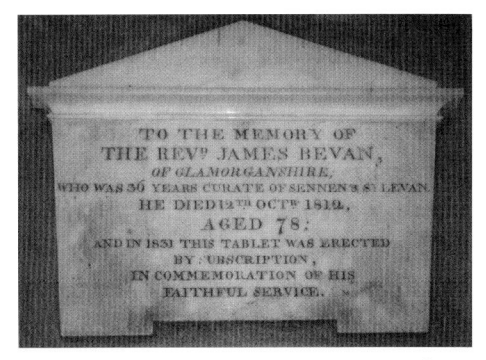

Memorial to the Revd James Bevan, curate of St Levan and Sennen for a record 36 years (the rector was the absentee Dean of St Buryan). Many curates found St Levan too challenging, but James, perhaps because he came from a similar environment, clearly loved the parish and was loved in return.

Bevan saw three Deans in post, the third being **Henry Jenkin** (Dean 1799-1817). His beginnings (in Westwick in Norfolk) seem to have been more humble than some of his predecessors', but he was clever and hard-working and became a Fellow of St John's in 1756, and was made DD in 1792. He too was a pluralist, holding various rectorships in Sussex and then Northamptonshire before also becoming Dean of St Buryan in 1799. In 1808, he resigned his Northamptonshire livings for presumably more lucrative ones in Surrey, and in 1810 acquired a prebend at Winchester. He held these posts until his death just before Christmas, 1817,[137] enjoying their considerable income, and never coming to St Buryan, let alone St Levan. Crofts wrote:

> During his incumbency conditions, if possible, went from bad to worse. A writer to the *West Briton* on 20th January 1814 complains that Sennen and St Levan had no curates and that no services had been performed there since October.[138]

What had been happening?

After James Bevan's death in 1812, there was a gap before a replacement was found. The new man when he came was **William Vawdrey** (1771-1838), but he stayed only a short time, leaving early in 1814 for a curacy at Gwinear. Judging by his reputation there, this was a great loss to St Levan.[139] His replacement was **Charles Henry Paynter**: his name appears in the Buryan Book as curate, but that is all. His rapid disappearance from the local scene is the reason for the gross neglect of St Levan mentioned in the *West Briton*.

At last, in 1815, a replacement was found: **William Spry**, who was still a young man at the time of his appointment – he was born in about 1790 and had only graduated the previous year – from Exeter College, Oxford. William Bottrell, writing half a century after Spry had left the area, said that he "must still be well remembered by man in town and country," and described his "harmless whims" and "eccentric vagaries." He lived well away from here, in Penzance, and would visit his cure only when the weather was good enough – and it was not often good enough. From time to time he did make his way west – most notably on his "wooden horse", a velocipede, a wooden tricycle, propelled by the rider's feet on the ground. There are several stories of how he terrorized the neighbourhood without losing the affection of those who knew him. Whether the women whose eggs and butter were hurled into the river when he crashed into them one market-day were so forgiving is unlikely. It is said, indeed, that they nearly killed him, and that he was lucky to be rescued by some passing gentlemen.

Come the following Sunday the path to St Levan Church up Rospletha Hill from Bodellan (this is before Porthcurno was developed) was full of people wanting to see the wounded parson. Had he turned up, he might have had one of the biggest congregations St Levan had seen in a good while: but, alas! he did not. He tried to come the next Sunday, but he and the velocipede ended up in a muddy hole.[140]

In 1827, Spry became Rector of Botus Fleming, up on the border with Devon,[141] where he entertained the locals as thoroughly as he had in Penwith, poking fun at the pompous, and telling tall tales starring himself; he died there in 1844.

Less than two years after Spry came to Penzance, Dean Jenkin died, and

Fitzroy Henry Richard Stanhope became Dean. He was the last Dean, although that was not evident until 1850, when the Act was passed to abolish the Deanery when he relinquished it (which he did only by dying, 14 years later). There is a great deal to say about Dean Stanhope, so much indeed that there will have to be a separate booklet devoted to his extraordinary life: extraordinary, that is, for a 19th-century Anglican clergyman. For a not-very-bright younger son of an 18th-century earl, his life was unremarkable. Regrettably, the delightful tales told about how he was appointed to the Deanery are not true: for example the alleged correspondence between the Duke of York and the Bishop of Cork ("Dear Cork, Please ordain Stanhope, Yours York"; "Dear York, Stanhope is ordained, Yours Cork") is apocryphal.[142] But rest assured that the truth is just as good.

For now, suffice it to say that Dean Stanhope never came to St Buryan. His income from the Deanery was over £1,000 per annum, from which he paid (most years) two curates about £100 each. Crofts estimated that over the 47 years of his tenure, Stanhope gained £60,000 from the Deanery tithes. He also held two livings in Yorkshire, which together brought in nearly £600 a year. There is however no evidence to suggest that he ever did a hand's turn as a priest, and there is no sign of his even having had a proper education.

St Levan knew of him as the man who, on Christmas Day 1820, farmed out his tithes for £250 pa (but not the fees from "marriages, christenings &c") to a consortium of local farmers and landed gentry, including Richard Hodge, Thomas Ellis, Thomas Roberts, Joseph Roberts, William Vingoe Bottrell and Joseph Roberts "of Helston gentleman"; and who 21 years later bought the tithes back, paying 10s each to the surviving "farmers." For the duration of the agreement, the "farmers" were responsible for the upkeep of the chancel, while Stanhope remained responsible for paying the curate.[143]

When the amusing Mr. Spry left for the banks of the Tamar at Botus Fleming, in 1827, **Edward Cox** got the job. He left in 1829. His successor, after another pause, was **William Woodis Harvey**, who stayed an even shorter time – a scant year – but much more is known about him. He was born in Penzance in 1798 and educated there; he became a Wesleyan missionary in Haiti in his early twenties and lived there for some six years. On his return he wrote about his experiences in *Sketches of Hayti from the Expulsion of the French to the*

Death of Christophe (1827, still in print in the USA for black-studies courses), but not before he had married Sarah Morgan, also of Penzance. Encouraged by his rich friend CV Le Grice, the perpetual curate at St Mary's, Penzance, Harvey went to Cambridge, and by 1828 had his BA; in the same year he became curate at St Mary's, presumably assisting Le Grice. He then came to St Levan and Sennen for his short year: as a local man he will have known about the problems of the Deanery, exacerbated by its new, even laxer Dean, and he may have wished to help rescue the situation. But he too did not tarry; his next post seems to have been King Charles the Martyr, Falmouth.

Next came **George Pigott** (curate from 1831 to 1833 or '34): yet another short-term post-holder. He is remembered in St Levan, if at all, as the co-discoverer of the mineral pigotite at Cripp's Cove below the Logan Rock. Modern mineralogy doubts whether it is a distinct species, but it remains on the records.[144] He was the librarian of the Royal Geological Society of Cornwall, a post he presumably gave up when he left to be an East India Company chaplain at Bombay in 1834. He stayed there until 1850, and his life may well be worth further research. **Samuel Lowthrop** was the next curate, for less than a year (1834).

The curate following provides us, at last, with some clues about the reasons for this rapid turnover: **John Daniel** (curate here 1834-37) printed the farewell sermon he gave in June 1837 at both St Levan and Sennen churches. In the preamble he wrote of the "arduous situation" in which he had been placed:

> Many are the discouragements . . . I have met with, – some of them connected with even the decent performance of our public worship; others, with the various departments of parochial and ministerial superintendance: – but I forebear to enumerate, lest I should appear to reproach.[145]

It is clear from Daniel's account that it was Henry Phillpotts (Bishop of Exeter 1830-69) who had placed him in the "arduous situation" of St Levan and Sennen – not the Dean. Phillpotts had clearly intervened to make up for the Dean's neglect. And there is other evidence of Phillpotts' having a say in Deanery affairs: there survive some chits of his giving Dean Stanhope leave-of-absence from his cure.[146]

Daniel also had a problem with the Methodists. His reference to the need for "strict and conscientious communion with the Established Church" is aimed at them, and he is quite explicit about the threat they posed to his cure. Fourteen years later, the Ecclesiastical Census of 1851[147] underlined it:

Ecclesiastical Census of 1851: entries for St Levan			
	Morning	Afternoon	Evening
St Levan Church		22 Sunday scholars	
Sowah Chapel Wesleyan			75
Bottoms Wesleyan		100	
Treen Chapel Wesleyan			119

On the Sunday in question, there were no services at all at St Levan Church, just a Sunday School in the afternoon, which 22 children attended; by contrast, there were 294 attendances at Wesleyan chapels. Even taking the Wesleyan figures with a pinch of salt, the contrast is stark.

Charles Jenkyns (curate 1837-46) stuck it out for nine years. He was a St Ives man (born c1804), and thus presumably knew what he was letting himself in for. He lived in Sennen Churchtown, and his two children, Charles and Blanch, were born there in about 1840 and 1843 respectively.[148] Daniel had left him congregations "steadily, though slowly, on the increase, in both churches"[149] and he may have been able to build on that.

One important event took place during Jenkyns' curacy: the commutation of the tithes to an agreed cash equivalent. St Levan's turn was in 1838: the survey confirmed that all the tithes belonged to the Dean as Rector of St Buryan — rectors by definition owned both great and small tithes. (Great tithes were of corn and other grains, and of hay and wood, the small tithes being everything else.) In St Levan, this amounted to a cash value of £250 a year, payable by the landowners to the Dean and his successors. The two richest men in the parish (Richard Hodge and Joseph Roberts) paid 20 percent of the tithes, which explains the interest of the Hodge and Roberts families in being churchwardens and thus having some control over the disbursement of parish funds.

Charles Jenkyns left the Deanery in 1846 to become curate of Helston;[150] in 1853 he became the Vicar of All Saints, Tuckingmill, where he remained until his death in 1875.[151]

H Walter Phillips was another who stayed but a year (1846-47). In July of 1847 he moved to Chacewater, but on 10th May 1848 he was one of six passengers killed in the GWR railway accident at Shrivenham, when a train collided with a horse-box at the station.[152]

Meanwhile his successor at St Levan was already about to move on. **George Rundle Prynne** was in his day the most famous man to have been curate here although, as usual, his fame came later. His father was from Newlyn, but George was born in West Looe, Cornwall. When he was priest in Bristol, he met Edward Pusey, and became a Tractarian – that is, he espoused the high-church ideas and practices associated by many with Roman Catholicism. When his father died in 1847, he was deeply distressed and applied for a move from his current living in Par. Dr. Phillpotts proposed St Levan as a temporary post "until something could be found better suited to your talents and energies." Prynne must have regretted the change almost immediately: although he "enjoyed the wild romantic scenery of the Cornish coast, and spent much leisure-time climbing and sketching... he felt the loneliness of the place, the remoteness of which was at that time far greater than it now is."[153] Prynne soldiered on:

> Congregations of half a dozen or less at either of the two churches; four communicants only on Christmas Day; services to which no one came, – conditions like these were disheartening indeed. Yet his diary shows that he plodded on, starting Sunday schools, teaching the children on week-days – for there was no day-school in the place then—and doing what he could to improve the character of the services....[154]

By July 1848, Bishop Phillpotts took pity on Mr. Prynne and moved him to St Peter's, Plymouth, where he spent the rest of his life, dying there in 1903. He continued to be the centre of theological storms, and rode out riots – something he had been spared at St Levan – but it was clearly far more to his taste than the Land's End.

The next curate seems to have been happier; one hopes so, as he was here for 16 years. **William Houghton** was born in about 1813 in Preston, Lancashire. He lived in Sennen Churchtown, apparently in lodgings with

Roodscreen image 5: These may be wyverns again, but they both have four feet, which usually signifies a dragon. However, the fact that the creature on the left apparently has a head at each end may account for that. And perhaps we should be careful not to assume too much knowledge about these beasts on the part of the carvers! (For more about wyverns and images of them at St Levan church, see illustrations on page 12.)

The stained glass window on south wall of the Lady Chapel: This is "in loving memory of Henry Hodge of Bosistow in this parish," who died in 1921, and was erected by his widow. It shows to the left St George, holding a sword; on the right, St Michael, holding a pair of scales to weigh the souls of the departed; and in the middle Christ as the Light of the World. The window-cill beneath was given in 1948 by Rowena Cade (founder of the Minack Theatre), in memory of her mother, Mary Cade (1858-1946), for whose soul we are asked to pray.

Richard and Martha Botheras by their carpenter's workshop.[155] He was a minor author, and during his time here wrote several articles for the *Ecclesiastic*, a Tractarian periodical. These reflected his lifelong interest in refuting Calvinist doctrines, emphasizing what he saw as the misguided beliefs of Methodists. He also had a speech of his printed: *The Duty of renewed zeal and exertions in the service of our country ... recommended in an address to the Duke of Cornwall's [10th] Volunteer Artillery Corps, etc.*[156] This Corps was raised at Buryan on 5th November 1860 as part of the new Cornwall Artillery Volunteers;[157] and William Houghton was there to encourage the young men of his parishes to sign up.

This is the last glimpse we have of a curate of St Levan and Sennen in the Deanery.

Houghton was appointed Vicar of Manaccan (on the Lizard) when the Deanery disappeared, and he lived there until his death in 1870.

✢ ✢ ✢ ✢ ✢

The end of the Deanery and the creation of the Rectorship
A Considerable Scandal

In 1850, a Bill was successfully presented to the House of Lords "to divide the Deanery of St Burian." Lord Portman introduced it by remarking on the "dilapidated and mutilated condition of St Burian and the other two churches." The proposal was similar to that of the Chantry Commissioners some 300 years earlier: to establish a rectory in each parish; to make the rectors subject to the jurisdiction of the Bishop of Exeter; and to abolish the Deanery Court. None of this would happen until the present Dean either resigned or died. His Lordship concluded:

> The advantage likely to be derived from the proposed changes generally can scarcely be over-estimated, calculated, as they would be, most materially to improve the condition of the population, and at the same time remove a considerable scandal, detrimental to the Church not only in the deanery itself, but in the surrounding vicinity. The abolition of the registry court would relieve the inhabitants from what is considered a great grievance and abuse.[158]

Dean Stanhope had a thick skin. He did not resign, and he seems not to have changed his habits.

A new church for St Levan?

The first Rector of St Levan was **Joseph Sidney Tyack** (sometimes spelled Tyacke). His mother was Catherine, daughter of Joseph Roberts, formerly of Roskestal, in St Levan (above Porthgwarra). Roberts was a former churchwarden and one of the great landowners of the parish. As "Joseph Roberts of Helston gentleman," he had been one of the consortium which farmed Dean Stanhope's tithes from 1820.[159] Tyack, named for his maternal grandfather, was born in 1835 in Helston;[160] he came to St Levan in 1864 from Marlborough College where he had been an assistant master after graduating from Exeter College Oxford. It was a good posting for a 29-year-old and perhaps due to the memory of his grandfather. He lived over at Roskestal (or "Roscastle" as he put it[161]) where his grandfather had been born and where cousins of his still farmed. According to Burr, he introduced singing into services, and set up a choir, buying members' surplices out of his "not insubstantial" income.

He also wrote and published a pamphlet on one of the burning issues of the day: the election of bishops[162] – a system which he described as "a solemn, profane and wicked farce," and which was under attack because of an attempt to use it to prevent the election of Gladstone's nominee for the vacant see of Exeter, Frederick Temple (a future Archbishop of Canterbury). Mr. Tyack's paper was read at the Ruridecanal Synod of Penwith, and a copy was sent to every cathedral in the land, eliciting a reply in the *Contemporary Review* from the Dean of Ely.[163] It is not known what influence Tyack's article had, but Temple became Bishop of Exeter. At last St Levan was represented, and effectively, in its diocese.

Its church however was a problem: "Internally the building is in a most dilapidated and neglected state, extremely damp, and with the atmosphere of a vault."[164] Happily, the new (unmarried) Rector's priority was not building himself a Rectory, but "putting the Church in decent order for public worship, and [for] the better accommodation & comfort of the parishioners."[165]

The first meeting of the new Vestry Committee was on 18th April

1865, "in the Cottage adjoining the Church," but the meeting very soon adjourned (as it usually did) to the Logan Rock Inn to discuss: the election of churchwardens; the repair of the execrable Church-paths; and putting the Church in decent order. It was agreed that "a competent person be asked to make a Survey, & give in an estimate" of the cost of restoring the church.

The survey, by James St Aubyn (a well-known church architect and a member of the family at St Michael's Mount), decided the Rector against a restoration of the old church, for two reasons: one, access was difficult for everyone, and almost impossible "for aged & weakly persons;" and two, it would cost almost as much to repair the old church as to build a new one "in a central position."[166] He reported his decision in July 1866.

Opinion was divided, not least because of the expense. Methodists were understandably concerned that a compulsory rate should not be raised to pay for it. But Joseph Roberts of Raftra gave some land, at Tinpot Hill (now called Tippet Hill) in the middle of the parish, and promises of money were forthcoming: the motion to erect a new Church was carried by 11 to 7. By November, many subscriptions were in (some £350), and discussions were afoot about what other kind of help people were willing to provide.

The Rector wrote to the Incorporated Church Building Society (ICBS) seeking a grant. The form he filled in tells us that the old church had 170 paid seats in the nave and 30 free seats "in the Gallery" (the first floor of the tower). Mr. Tyack explained the need for a new building:

> The present Church is located quite away from the different villages – only one house is near it – …The bulk of the population is from 1 to 2½ miles distant – The player on the Harmonium, and his family and co-villagers, have if they attend both services to walk about 8 miles and, pass, through fields, over 104 stiles. There is no direct road to the Church, & only one by which it <u>can</u> be approached, around the exposed cliff.
>
> Till the Deanery was divided in 1864, the Church was served once on a Sunday, by a Curate living in the adjoining Parish – The Service was held alternately in the morning and afternoon – The square-pew accommodation, is monopolized to an extent which keeps people from the Church – There are 3 dissenting places of worship, and it is proposed to build a new one.

… There is a large Wesleyan School for the ordinary days of the week with a certificated Master – … the neighbouring Incumbent, … & myself have placed at the School an uncertificated Master, & retained our Mistress, whom we found at the School – The Scholars have very largely increased.

There is no Rectory. not house [sic] to be obtained for me. Neither is there any glebe. The Tithe Rent is commuted at 250£ per annum.[167]

Finally, making it even harder to raise money for this cause, local rates are much higher than usual because "the State of the Mines" is increasing costs at the workhouse (at Madron).

The ICBS decided to grant £50, which was high by standards. The new church was to have 257 seats, and to cost £1250.

But the new church was never built: why not? The main reason was that J. Sidney Tyack had become Vicar of Helston, losing St Levan the moving force behind the whole strategy.

There followed an unsettled period while a couple of curates filled the gap until a replacement was found. The new Rector, **Charles Christopher Anstey**, came in August 1868, and established himself at Burnewhall House in St Buryan parish with his wife Frances, their two children, Bessie and Harry, and a carriage. Maud was born a couple of years later.[168] CC Anstey, born in 1826, was the son of a master at Rugby School; he took his degree at Gonville & Caius at Cambridge and entered the church. In 1851 he was curate at Cleeve Prior in Worcestershire, but for much of the 1860s – immediately after the Mutiny – he was the Chaplain at Faizabad, in Oude, with his family.

Anstey did not want a new church for St Levan. In January 1869, he wrote to the ICBS that it had been "impossible to raise a sum sufficient to build a new Church in this Parish." The project had run out of steam and he was not going to waste any effort in reviving it.

The fate of the King Charles Board: a detective story

At the height of the first Civil War, in 1643, the King wrote a letter of thanks to the people of Cornwall from "his camp at Sudeley Castle," and at St Levan, as in many other parishes, the text was painted on a large board and hung in the church. You can still see the Boards — for example at Madron — but not at St Levan.

In 1866, the new rector wanted a new church, and the Vestry was desperately short of funds. At the beginning of August:

> the disposal of the Pieces of the King Charles' Board was next brought to the [Vestry] meeting, and Mrs. Dent's offer of 5£ in return for them announced — the wishes of the Parishioners were therefore consulted, and it appeared that there was no objection to their being parted with.[169]

And so it was that St Levan's King Charles Board left the parish, which was £5 the richer.

Who was Mrs. Dent? Where is the Board now?

In neither the 1861 nor the 1871 census were there any women called Dent living in Cornwall, so it was very likely that our Mrs Dent was a visitor: one of the 600 or 700 Mrs Dents elsewhere in England. I put the census to one side, and Googled: *The Annals of Winchcombe and Sudeley* by Emma Dent was published in 1877. Of the 46 Emma Dents in England in 1861, one was mistress of Sudeley Castle, which of course was where King Charles had written his Letter of Thanks. Emma Dent had been born Emma Brocklehurst in 1825 or 1826 in Macclesfield, the daughter of a prosperous silk manufacturer, and in 1847, Emma married John Coucher Dent, owner of the Castle and from the Worcester glove-making family: they began to restore the old house.

A quick e-mail to the archivist at Sudeley Castle revealed that there is a Charles I board on display in the Banqueting Hall, and that Emma Dent had bought it in 1862. But it came from Philleigh parish, not St Levan.

That is where the trail goes cold. Emma had written about acquiring the Board in *The Annals*,[170] and although her dates seem confused there is no reason to doubt its provenance. There is no record of the disposal of the St Levan pieces. Perhaps Mrs. Dent chose the best of her collection for display and disposed of the others before even leaving Cornwall. It may yet turn up.

✦ ✦ ✦ ✦

The Modern Parish(es)

"Putting the Church in Decent Order"

St Levan's ancient church had been reprieved, almost by chance, and efforts were now once more concentrated on "putting the Church in decent order for public worship, and [for] the better accommodation & comfort of the parishioners."[171] Unusually, no plans survive for the repairs and improvements which were carried out in these years, but presumably this was when the gallery was removed, and perhaps when the Dairy was brought back within the church.

Mr. Anstey turned to John Dando Sedding to design the work. JD Sedding had joined his brother Edmund's Penzance practice in 1865, at about the time Edmund's health failed; he moved away after Edmund's death in 1868, eventually setting up at 447 Oxford Street, in 1880, next door to Morris & Co. He was a disciple of Ruskin, believing architecture to be "not a commercial venture, but a divinely inspired art inseparable from handicraft."

He became a successful church architect, and "was a simple, impulsive, warm-hearted man with a sense of fun, who inspired undying devotion in his friends and pupils."[172] JD was responsible for most if not all the design work at Wendron, where Anstey's brother was Vicar, and the success of that work could well be why he got the St Levan job.

Bishop Temple of Exeter came for the re-opening of the Church, and there were refreshments after the ceremony in the barn at Rospletha. We know about the barn, because Mr. Joseph Hocking of Trendrennen told the Revd LA Tonkin about it in the 1930s: his father, Joseph Hocking of Rospletha, was a boy in the choir when Temple visited.[173] Mr. Hocking of Trendrennen's grandson, Barrie, farms today at Trengothal.

St Levan church and change
Shapurji Edalji

Overnight, in the spring of 1864, St Levan went from merely sharing a curate with Sennen, to having not only a Rector all to itself, but a curate too. This new task was very different from that which had driven curates only 20 years before close to despair.

Shapurji Edalji (1841/2–1918) was curate here in 1873-4. His name will be familiar to readers of Julian Barnes's *Arthur & George*, although there is nothing in the novel about St Levan.[174] Edalji (pronounced with the emphasis on the first syllable) was born in Bombay, the son of a Parsi merchant. He converted to Christianity and attended the Free Kirk College in about 1864, and in 1866 was given a licence to preach in Bombay. He then worked as a Presbyterian missionary among the Waralis, an aboriginal hill tribe of India. (The Waralis were said to worship "the lord of tigers in the form of a shapeless stone";[175] it would be interesting to know what Mr. Edalji made of the St Levan Stone!)

Edalji was a linguistic scholar: for example, he published a Gujarati/English dictionary (1863) and a Gujarati grammar (1867). In 1867 he travelled to England and studied at St Augustine's College, Canterbury, before being ordained deacon by Bishop Samuel Wilberforce of Oxford. The idea was that he would duly return to Bombay, to be priested and work as a colonial chaplain there. Mr. Edalji had other plans, and refused to go back to India. Wilberforce supported him, and he was ordained priest in the early 1870s in England, remaining here for the rest of his life.

After several other postings, he came to St Levan from 1873 to 1874, then moved on, and married Charlotte Stoneham, a vicar's daughter. His final curacy (1875-76) was at Bromley St Leonard, in east London. In 1876, he became Vicar of Great Wyrley (near Walsall), where he served for 42 years until his death in 1918. He and Charlotte had three children, one of them the George of *Arthur & George*. The *ODNB* describes the Revd Shapurji as "an amiable, devoted clergyman."

But the reason he is in the *ODNB*, and the reason Julian Barnes wrote his novel, is the racial prejudice which he and his family suffered. The appalling story is too complex to relate here (read the novel!), but it is hard to imagine that he or his family were ever happy again once the harassment began in 1888, even after Conan Doyle's efforts restored some of the son's reputation. We can only hope that Shapurji was happy at St Levan. There is a reference to him in the diary of a senior officer of the telegraph company, George Spratt, who was also a churchwarden: "1874, January 15: Met Rev Edaly [sic] at Mansell's."[176] And that is all.

The Eastern Telegraph Company

I suspect that the reason St Levan Church was restored despite the earlier lack of funds was because the Eastern Telegraph Company made up the shortfall. George Spratt's diary, for example, refers to discussions about finances with ETC management, and the Company clearly played a major part in the church throughout its time in the Porthcurno valley. When the Station closed, Cable & Wireless Ltd (successors to Eastern Telegraph) presented the church with a bible "to commemorate an association of over 100 years with that company's branch at Porthcurno."[177]

The impact of the ETC on St Levan was enormous: in 1861 about 90 per cent of the population (406 people) were from either St Levan or a parish very close by; in 1871 there were 20 people directly employed by or training with ETC, none of them from Penwith; in 1881 there were 35; in 1891, 48; and in 1901, 128. The bleakness which had so haunted those isolated curates two decades earlier must have been much mitigated by the social and intellectual variety introduced by all these telegraphic and electrical students and clerks who thronged into the church, and sang in choir, and built a theatre in the valley ... One imagines that the young St Levan male was not as happy about this as his sister was.

George Spratt began at the Station in 1871 as Chief Clerk, and eventually became Assistant Superintendent. For many years he kept a diary, which is now in Porthcurno Museum. It is of interest here not just for the mention of Edalji, but because for many years he was a churchwarden at St Levan, and his diary gives a flavour of what that entailed, and of the problems, scandals, difficulties and delights involved.

There is room here for only a brief taste, taking a year at random: 1877, a year which saw the deaths of two important people in St Levan life. First was Joseph Roberts of Raftra who died in June, aged 82 or so: the man who had offered land for the new parish church ten years before, and one of the richest men in St Levan. Four months later, the diary tells us that his family left Raftra; and a fortnight later, the Revd Charles Anstey died. Burr's *History* says that he died in the parish, but that cannot be right: not only did George Spratt not know about it for a week, but Anstey's death was registered in Fulham, London. It does look from Spratt's diary as though Mr. Anstey had been away from the parish for some time, and that fellow clergymen were helping out in the meantime – especially Mr. Bennett. This will be Trimer Bennett, who 11 years later was to become Rector here.

A rectory for St Levan

Anstey's successor was the Revd **Paul d'Ockham Silvester**, who was inducted on 7th May 1878.[178] He was born in about 1827 in Somerset, the son of a successful physician, who soon moved his family to London. Paul was an MA of Exeter College, Oxford (1850): he held five curacies, mainly in the west country, before coming to St Levan as Rector, where he settled into a cottage with a housekeeper (Elizabeth Clark Stevens, of Paul) and a servant. His immediate priority was not a Rectory, but a proper Sunday school.

A site was eventually found in Porthcurno (now rivalling Treen in size), and on 23rd September 1882, Benjamin Thomas, a St Buryan builder, was engaged "to build a School Room, privies etc. at Porthcurno, according to plan and specification, for the sum of two hundred and 40 pounds."[179] The final settlement with the builder was made in 1888, although there is no sign of what took so long.[180] Just before the turn of the century, there is a sad footnote: a reference to the schoolroom as "very badly kept, & often not fit to use. It is more or less a White Elephant…."[181]

In 1895, 17 years after Silvester's arrival, Lord St Levan gave an acre of land in the Churchtown for a rectory. Two problems soon emerged: one was access to water (which the tenant of the rest of the field was obstructing) and then it emerged that the plans for the house and gardens took rather more than the donated acre.[182] All of this was sorted out, and then things went quiet again. Building probably began; but then the Rector retired to Penzance, in 1898, where he lived as a boarder in Miss Stevens' house. He died in Penzance in 1908, aged 80.

Trimer Bennett was a very different man from his predecessor. Where Silvester had been the son of a comfortably-off doctor, Bennett was the son of a college servant in Cambridge. In 1861 he was assistant to the Headmaster of Bath Grammar School, and that summer he married Ellen Jane Tudor Palmer, a governess. By 1871, Trimer was living in Penrose Terrace in Penzance, with wife, mother-in-law, sister-in-law, several school-boy boarders, and four young children of his own. He was apparently headmaster of Penzance Grammar School from 1861, but at some point he took holy orders: in 1871 he was also curate of St Just as well. It is said that he closed the grammar school in the 1890s, and opened a private school; he closed this too when he went to St Levan. In the 1891 census, he gives his occupation as "Clerk in Holy Orders; Domestic Chaplain to Lord St Levan, St Michael's Mount…" We also know that he stood in for Mr. Anstey 20 years before; when Mr. Silvester went on a continental tour in March and April 1880, he officiated.[183] When Mr. Silvester retired, he got the job.

His family was grown by then, but he had a wife and he was used to the domestic comforts. They were dismayed at what they found. There was no door on the coal shed and no picture rails in the house; the drainage system was illegal and required improvement, including a cesspit; and so on, and on. The sewage work took up nearly all the available funds.[184] A somewhat exasperated Lord St Levan refused the extra land. When Mr. Bennett asked for Venetian blinds in the house, a firm line was drawn. Nor would the St Levan churchwardens pay.

Some how or other, the matter was resolved; but it was a sad start to the new Rectory, and to Mr Bennett's time here. Perhaps he was not an easy man to get on with: I have been told that he once refused to take the funeral service of a parishioner because the congregation was a few minutes late. They were late because they had had to carry the coffin along the church-paths from Trengothal, but the Rector was unimpressed, although he did perform the service in the end. And my same informant tells another story of her Methodist father being given pennies by the kindly Rector.

He was Rector until his death in February 1925, aged 82 or 83.

The next Rector was **Henry Tristram Valentine** (1857-1941). Already in his seventies, he had had a varied and demanding life. He was born in Kensington on 10th June 1857, the third and youngest son of a civil engineer. He attended Trinity College Cambridge (1875-78), and originally intended to be a lawyer (as one of his brothers was), but he was ordained deacon at Durham in 1880.

He became curate of Fulham (1882-5), and then Chaplain at the London Hospital (1885-9) – but this job ended badly and he resigned. In 1890, he appeared as a witness before a House of Lords Committee on Metropolitan Hospitals, testifying about the poor training conditions for nurses at the London Hospital, the misleading nature of its advertising, and the inefficient (not to say despotic) management style of the Matron, the famous Eva Lückes (1854-1919). He was by no means alone in his complaints, but the Committee eventually found "not only the charges to be unsubstantiated but that the majority of the allegations were exaggerated."

Even worse, he had had to defend himself publicly about the reasons for his resignation: there had been allegations that he had brought pressure to bear on nurses to take confession, and that he had refused them communion if they did not. An ecclesiastical report into his conduct had exonerated him from charges, but (he said) he had not been told the result of the enquiry, and he had resigned.

Be that as it may, at the time of his resignation, he already had another job lined up, as Vicar of St Paul's Walden, Hertfordshire (1889-1906). By now he and his wife Ellen had three daughters, as well a governess, nurse, cook and house-maid. It was while he was working here that he baptised the future Queen Elizabeth the Queen Mother, an event which was affectionately recalled many years later. In November 1937, during a visit of the then King and Queen to St Paul's Walden, her Majesty unveiled a tablet in the church to commemorate both the Coronation and her birth in the parish; during the same service the now 80-year-old Mr Valentine dedicated the new electric organ.

He left St Paul's Walden in 1906 to become Vicar of St Bene't and All Saints, Kentish Town, and then to Egypt to be the Chaplain in Ramleh. During this time, the First World War broke out, and in 1915 he joined the Royal Army Chaplain's Department and served there until 1919. There is then a gap in the record: he was over 60 and had been through the war, so perhaps he tried retirement. But from 1923 he was Warden of the Clergy House of Rest at West Malvern, which he left in 1926 to come to St Levan as Rector.[185]

On 9th March 1932, just a few months before he retired, Mr Valentine was in St Just playing bridge with friends. His wife was at home, it being the evening for the weekly sewing class at the Rectory. What happened next is still remembered by some parishioners: the mother of one of them worked at the Rectory before her marriage. This was Dorothy Semmens, whose son Ken Chiffers is the chief source for this story, as told to Christine Gendall. The attic was heated by a paraffin stove which someone forgot to turn off at the end of the sewing meeting, and perhaps a draught blew the curtains into the flame: "a fire ensued."

> The fire brigade was summoned from Penzance. At this time the tyres of the engine were solid and progress to the fire was slow. Ken relates that they were also slowed by the fact that the firemen did not know the route to St Levan Church and had to stop to ask for directions on the way. They had been told that it was near the Coastguard houses at Treen. By the time they arrived at the Rectory the fire had burned to the ground floor. Ken suspects that there may not have been a ready source of water for the brigade to use.[186]

Miss Semmens was engaged to be married: her trousseau was destroyed in the fire, as possibly also was her engagement ring, but she was married on 12th October 1932 at St Levan by Mr. Valentine.

Another story says that a messenger rushed to St Ives to tell the Rector that his house was burning down, but his response (once he knew that no one had been hurt) was that he was sure that his wife was quite capable of coping without him, especially as there were servants and family there to help. He eventually made his way home "to find that his faith in his family was completely justified."[187] The resourceful Mrs. Valentine had been Ellen

St Levan rectory after the fire in March 1932: This blurred newspaper photograph underlines the bleakness of the scene on the morning after. Not only was the Valentines' home destroyed, but the Rectory was gone. For centuries St Levan had been a dependent chapel of St Buryan, only from 1864 an independent parish, and with a Rectory building only from about 1898. And here it is in ruins. (It was rebuilt, and is now a private home.) *With thanks to Christine Gendall.*

Barlow, and they had married in 1880. They must have had private means from the start: even in his first post, they were well enough off to have a cook and maid living in, not a usual curate's household!

HT Valentine left here in 1932, retiring to Lelant, where he died on 13th February 1941.

Plus ça change....

In 1932, **Lancelot Arthur Tonkin** became Rector, to whom thanks are due from anyone interested in the history of this parish, for he began the invaluable Scrapbook. He was also the Rector who undertook the transformation of the west end of the south aisle into the Lady Chapel. His grandfather was Uriah Tonkin, who from 1814 to 1841 had been curate of St Buryan, under the two last Deans, Henry Jenkins and Fitzroy Stanhope, and for at least some of the grim time when St Levan was having such problems attracting and retaining curates. From 1919 to 1923, the Revd Lancelot Tonkin had been Curate at St Mary's Bromley St Leonard – where some 45 years before, Shapurji Edalji had been curate: it would be nice to think that he knew of this connexion.

William George Hills, like his two most recent predecessors, had been a Chaplain to the Forces during World War I, though unlike them, he had spent the war in Australia.

Charles Leslie Abdy (Rector 1956-62) shared Lancelot Tonkin's interest in the history of the parish, adding to the Scrapbook and helping to preserve documents.

Maurice Furlonger (Rector 1962-66) left when the parish was joined with St Buryan: and the new Rector of the joint parishes was the man who had previously been at St Buryan alone – **Hugh Fryer**. He in turn left when Sennen was added in 1972, and **Maurice Friggens** became Rector of the three parishes. The irony of the three parishes of the Deanery being re-united was not lost on anyone, although the advantages of the new arrangement (which had nothing else in common with the old Deanery!) were clear. Church congregations were small, and candidates for the priesthood rarer: the old system was too expensive.

Since then, there have been two Rectors: **Richard Legg** (1985-1994) and **Aelred Harry Burlton** (1994-2005); **Brin Berriman** was appointed Priest-in-Charge in 2005. The difference between rectors and priests-in-charge is that rectors have a freehold on their position: they cannot be moved without their consent unless they behave very badly indeed – not that this has happened in St Levan (at least not for a 150 years!). Having instead a priest-in-charge thus makes planning far easier – because the Bishop will be able to make better use of the resources in the diocese. Eventually, these three parishes, together with St Just, Pendeen, Sancreed and Morvah, will be served by two stipendiary priests, where at the moment there are three.

History does not stop. St Levan and its church will continue to change. Congregations are still small, but they are devoted, and St Levan Church has been well looked after of late years. Your purchase of this book helps to preserve this small gem for future generations, and for this, and your interest in its history, we thank you.

Appendix A: List of Clergy

Known St Levan Clergy & Deans of St Buryan

NB: The Prebendaries of Trethyn (Treen) drew their stipends from land thought to be in St Levan, but they otherwise had no direct connexion with the parish.

Date	Prebendary of Trethyn	Dean of St Buryan	Monarch
1213, Feb 12		Walter de Gray	1199–1216, John
1214, Feb 7		William Provost of St Omer	1216–1272, Henry III
1220		William de Sancto Albino (St Aubyn)	
1259 July		Arnold, or Arnulf	
1269		Stephen Hayme	
Before 1272 to 1290?		John Kirkby	1272–1307, Edward I
1288	Hugo Splot		
1291	Davit de Ballec		
1300		William de Hameldone	
1302		Ralph de Manton	
1303		Matthew de Medentor or Medunta (i.e., Mantes) or de Boileaux	
1307	Peter-dictus-Perot (*Peter-called- Pierrot*)		1307–1327, Edward II
1318	Richard de Bello Prato (aka *Beaupré*)		
1318		John de Maunte (or de Medinta or Medunta)	1327–1377, Edward III

1329	Richard de Bello Prato (aka *Beaupré*) [reinstated]		
1337		Thomas de Cruce	
1338		John de Hale	
1339		Galfrido in Venella de Tadelawe	
1345		[Deanery seized as held by an alien.]	
1343	John Coke		
1348	David Botilet		
1349, 12 Oct		Richard de Wolveston	
1352, 12 Sep		John de Sancey	
1353, 21 June		David Macgnard *or* Maignard *or* Maynard	
1366	Robert de Stoner(e)		1377–1399, Richard II
1381, possibly 1363 16 Apr		Alan de Stokes	
1394, 1 Jan		John Boor	
1394		Nicholas Slake	1399–1413, Henry IV
1410	William Lockhard		1413–1422, Henry V,
1410		William Lochard	1422–1461, 1470–1471, Henry VI
1427		William Lord of Charde	
1438		Adam Moleyns	
1439		Peter Stucle	

1453	Henry Gorlyng		1461–1470, 1471–1483, Edward IV
1462, 20 Feb		Robert Knollys	
1473	John Howyll		
1478	John Co(o)mbe		1483, Edward V; 1483–1485, Richard III
1484	Nicholas Gosse		
1485	William Sylke		1485–1509, Henry VII; 1509–1547, Henry VIII
1509-22		John Ryse	
c 1530-1550	William Alsa (chaplain)	Dr. Thomas Bagh	
1535	John Westcot		
1536	John Byase		
1545	William Woodward		
	Prebends abolished		
	Curates to serve the Chapelry of St Levan	Dean	1547–1553, Edward VI; 1553, Jane; 1553–1558, Mary I; 1558–1603, Elizabeth I
1578, 28 Nov		William Fairchild	
?		John Gayer	
1592		William Forth	
?			
16…		Richard Murry	1603–1625, James I 1625–1649, Charles I

1635?1637?		Walter Ralegh *or* Rawleigh	
1637?1646?		Robert Creighton	
1642, 21 May	Symon William		
1646		John Weeks	1653-1658, Oliver Cromwell
1656-62	Joseph Hull		1658–1659, Richard Cromwell; 1660–1685, Charles II
1663		Seth Ward	
1667		Anthony Sparrow	
1676		Thomas Lamplugh	
1685	Nicholas Orchard		1685-1689, James II
1685		Sir John (Jonathan) Trelawney	1689-1702, William (III) & Mary (II) [Mary d 1694]
1693	William Polkinghorn		
1697	John Bagwell		1702–1714, Anne
1705	James Trenhaile William Buckenham		
1706	Joseph Jane		
1707		Ofspring Blackall	
1709	Thomas Paynter		
1714-30	John Clode		1714–1727, George I
1716		John Harris	

1716			1727–1760, George II
1728	Robert Corker		
1738-49	Jonathan Toup		
1739, 28 Feb		Arthur Ashley Sykes	
1750-53	John Borlase		
1754-69	Richard Pearce		
1756		Nicholas Boscawen	1760–1820, George III (from 1801, the Regency of his son)
1770-75	George Hawkins		
1775-1812	James Bevan		
1793, Oct		Samuel Alford	
1799		Henry Jenkins	
1812-14	William Vanday/Vawdrey		
1814	Charles Henry Paynter		
1815	William Spry		
1817		Fitzroy Henry Richard Stanhope	1820–1830, George IV
1827	Edward Cox		
1830	William Woodis Harvey		1830–1837, William IV
1831	George Piggott		
1834	Samuel Lowthrop		
1834	John Daniel		

1837	Charles Jenkyns		1837–1901, Victoria
1846	H. Walter Phillips		
1847	George Rundle Prynne		
1848	William Houghton		
Deanery of St Buryan abolished 1850; into effect 1864			
	Rector	Curate (where known)	
1864	Joseph Sydney Tyack		
1868		Henry Mansell (temp)	
1868		Frank Beadel (temp)	
1868	Charles Christopher Anstey		
1873-74		Shapurji Edalji	
20th May 1878	Paul d'Ockham Sylvester		
Sept 1898	Trimer Bennett		1901–1910, Edward VII; 1910–1936, George V
1926	Henry Tristram Valentine		
1932	Lancelot Arthur Tonkin		1936, Edward VIII; 1936–1952, George VI
1943	William George Hills		
1956	Charles Abdy		1952-, Elizabeth II
1962	Maurice F Furlonger		

	Rector of the combined parishes of St Buryan and St Levan		
1966	(Peter) Hugh Fryer		
	Rectors of the combined parishes of St Buryan, St Sennen and St Levan		
1972	Maurice Friggens	Trevor Cooke, Peter Rose, Geoffrey Stanley Johnston	
1985	Dr. Richard Legg		
1994	Aelred Harry Burlton		
	Priest-in-Charge of the combined parishes of St Buryan, St Sennen and St Levan		
2005	Brin Berryman		

Appendix B: Details of More Recent Incumbents

Biographical details of the more recent Rectors of St Levan (latterly, Priests-in-Charge)

Lancelot Arthur Tonkin (1882-19??)		
Born	1882	Madron, Cornwall
Education	1910	Theological Department, King's College London
Ordained d & p	1910, 1910	
Married	1912	Lucy Dorothea Fenn
Curate	1912-13	St Mary's, Par
	1913-19	St. Fimbarrus, Fowey
Chaplain	1917-19	Temporary Chaplain to the Forces
Curate	1919-23	St Mary's Bromley St Leonard
Vicar	1923-30	St Edward King and Martyr, Holbeck, Leeds
Curate	1930-32	Basingstoke
Rector	**1932-43**	St Levan

William George Hills (18??-19??)		
Education	1906	Theological Department, King's College London
Ordained d & p	1906, 1907	
Curate	1906-08	St Luke Victoria Docks, South Canning Town, east London
	1908-11	St John Baptist, Southend-on-Sea
Rector	1911-16	Bowen, north Queensland, Australia
Chaplain	1914-18	Temporary Chaplain to the Forces
Vicar	1918-21	St Michael's, Spennithorne, West Riding of Yorkshire
	1921-43	St Stithian with Perranarworthal
Rector	**1943-56**	St Levan

Charles Leslie Abdy (1897-19??)

Born	1897	Burton-on-Trent
Parents		Charles W Abdy, manager of a hat shop in that town, and his wife Annie
War	1914-20	There is a medal record for a Chas L Abdy, acting corporal
Education	1929	Lincoln Theological College
Ordained d & p	1931, 1932	
Curate	1931-33	St Saviour's Denmark Park, Camberwell, south London
	1933-35	Master at St Saviour's College, Carshalton, Surrey
	1933-37	Organizing Secretary of the Bishop of Southwark's Council for Work among Adolescents
	1935-37	Church of the Ascension, Balham Hill, south London
	1937-41	Caterham
Vicar	1941-53	St James Malden
Rector	1953-56	St Mawgan with St Martin-in-Meneage, Cornwall
Rector	1956-61	St Levan
Retired	1961	Morrab Road, Penzance

Maurice Frank Furlonger (1925-1999)

Born	1925	
Education	1950	Theological Department, King's College London
Ordained d & p	1951, 1952	
Curate	1951-1954	Hither Green, south London
Chaplain	1954-57	RAF
Vicar	1957-62	Fillongley, Warwickshire
Rector	1962-64	St Levan
	1964-67	Great Bookham, Surrey
Vicar	1967-70	St Minver, Cornwall
Vicar	1970-??	St Gluvias, Penryn, Cornwall

(Peter) Hugh Fryer (1925-2004)		
Born	1925	Burton-on-Trent
Education	1958	Lincoln Theological College
Ordained d & p	1960, 1961	
Curate	1960-64	Tavistock
Rector	1964-72	St Buryan
Rector	1966-72	St Levan
Rector	1972-76	Holy Trinity, Elgin, Moray (also Chaplain at RAF Lossiemouth)
Priest-in-Charge	1976-78	Lewannick
Team Rector	1978-84	Lewannick, Altarnun & Bolventor & North Hill
Rector & Prebendary	1984-90	St Endellion, with St Kew & Port Isaac

Maurice Anthony Friggens (1940-)		
Born	1940	
Education	1965	University of Sheffield (History)
Ordained d & p	1967, 1968	
Curate	1967-70	Stocksbridge, Sheffield
Curate	1970-72	St Buryan, St Levan & Sennen
Rector	1972-84	St Buryan, St Levan & Sennen
Rural Dean	1982	Penwith
Rector	1984-91	St Columb Major with St Wenn
Hon. Canon	1987	Truro Cathedral
Vicar	1991	St Cleve
Canon	1987-2000	St Columb
	2001	Retired to Wales

Richard Legg (1937-)		
Born	1937	
Education	1962 1963	Selwyn College Cambridge College of the Resurrection, Mirfield, West Yorkshire
Ordained d & p	1965, 1966	
Curate	1965-68	St Peter's Ealing
Chaplain	1968-78	Brunel University

Curate, then Team Vicar	1981-85	Chipping Barnet & Arkley
Rector	1985-93	**St Buryan, St Levan & Sennen**
Sub-warden	1993	St Deiniol's Library, Hawarden (Gladstone's Library)
Team Vicar	1993-97	Beaminster
Priest-in-Charge	1993-97	Veryan & Ruan Lanihorne

	Aelred Harry Burlton (1949-)	
Born	1949	
Education		Salisbury and Wells Theological College
Ordained d & p	1978, 1979	
Curate	1978-81	St Dunstan's, Feltham
	1982-94	C of E Chaplain at Heathrow Airport
Rector	**1994-2005**	**St Buryan, St Levan & Sennen**

	Brin Berriman	
Born	1950	St Ives
Education	1971	University College, London B. Sc. (1st class Hons) in Theoretical Physics
	1997	Certificate in Theology (Distinction), Exeter University
	1995-98	South West Ministerial Training Course
Other experience	1974-2000	Teaching mathematics in Penzance, latterly also college management
Ordained d & p	1998, 1999	
Curate	1998-2000	Non-stipendiary curate, St Ives and Halsetown
Priest-in-charge	2000-05	United Benefice of Lanteglos by Camelford with Advent
Priest-in-charge	**2005-**	**St Buryan, St Levan & Sennen**
Family		Married to Cheryl with 3 grown children

Appendix C: Discovering Church History

If you are interested in tracing the history of a Cornish church, the following sources may be of use.

Libraries and archives:

British Library Integrated Catalogue: http://catalogue.bl.uk.

Church of England Record Centre, Bermondsey, London (access via Lambeth Palace Library): www.lambethpalacelibrary.org/holdings/CERC.html.

Cornwall Record Office, Truro: www.cornwall.gov.uk/index.cfm?articleid=307; e-mail: cro@cornwall.gov.uk; tel: 01872-323127.

Cornish Studies Library, Redruth: www.cornwall.gov.uk/index.cfm?articleid=6773; e-mail: cornishstudies.library@cornwall.gov.uk; tel: 01209-216760.

Courtney Library, Royal Institution of Cornwall, Truro: www.royalcornwalmuseum.org.uk/pages/ric.1.asp?s=5&ss=1; e-mail: ric@royalcornwallmuseum.org.uk; tel: 01872-242786.

Devon Record Office, Exeter: www.devon.gov.uk/record_office.htm; e-mail: devrec@devon.gov.uk; tel: 01392-384253.

Exeter Cathedral Library and Archives, Exeter: www.exeter-cathedral.org.uk/Admin/Library.html; e-mail: library@exeter-cathedral.org.uk; tel: 01392-272894.

Lambeth Palace Library, London: www.lambethpalacelibrary.org e-mail: lpl.staff@c-of-e.org.uk; tel: 020 7898 1400.

Morrab Library, Penzance: http://morrablibrary.co.uk; e-mail: librarian@morrablibrary.co.uk; tel: 01736-364474.

The National Archives, Kew, London: www.nationalarchives.gov.uk; e-mail: via website; tel: 020 8876 3444.

Online resources:

"The Project Gutenberg EBook of *The Survey of Cornwall*, by Richard Carew," www.gutenberg.org/dirs/etext06/srvcr10.txt.
Celtic Christianity e-Library: www.lamp.ac.uk/celtic/ccelibrary.htm.
British History Online: www.british-history.ac.uk.
West Penwith Resources: http://west-penwith.org.uk/Levan.htm.

Printed books:

JT Blight, *Churches of West Cornwall – with notes of antiquities of the district* (London, 1865).
J. Caley (ed) *Valor Ecclesiasticus tempore Henrici VIII auctoritate regia institutus*, 6 vols (London, Record Commission, 1810-24).
William Copeland Borlase, *The Age of the Saints, a monograph of early Christianity in Cornwall* (Truro, 1893 [1st edn 1878]).
H Miles Brown, *The Church in Cornwall* (Oscar Blackford: Truro, 1964).
Len Burge, *Cornish Church Sundials* (Truro, 2002).
The Revd GH Doble, *Cornish Saints Series* (a reprint in 1997 of the 3rd [1938]edition).
Eamon Duffy, *The Voices of Morebath: Reformation and Rebellion in an English Village* (London, 2001).
FC Hingeston-Randolph, *The Register of John de Grandisson, Bishop of Exeter (AD 1327-1369)* (London and Exeter, 1897).
FC Hingeston-Randolph, *The Register of Walter de Stapeldon [sic], Bishop of Exeter (AD 1307-1326)* (London and Exeter, 1892).
FE Halliday. *A History of Cornwall* (London, 2000).
William Hals, *History of Cornwall* (Truro and Exeter, parts published in 1750, some unpublished and only available now in Polsue) www.west-penwith.org.uk/gulvalh.htm.
Charles Henderson, "The Ecclesiastical History of the 109 Parishes of West Cornwall", *JRIC* n.s. 2 (1953-6).
FE Howard, *The Mediæval Styles of the English Parish Church: a survey of their development, design and features* (London, 1936).
George Oliver, *Monasticon Dioecesis Exoniensis* (Exeter & London, 1846).
Richard Morris, *Churches in the Landscape* (London, 1997).

Elizabeth Okasha, *Corpus of Early Christian Inscribed Stones of South-west Britain* (London, 1993).

Lynette Olson, *Early Monasteries in Cornwall* (Woodbridge, 1989).

Nicholas Orme (ed) *Unity and Variety: A History of the Church in Devon and Cornwall* (Exeter, 1991).

Nicholas Orme, *Church Dedications in Cornwall* (Exeter, 1996).

Dorothy M Owen, *Records of the Established Church in England* (British Records Association, no 1; London, 1970).

Joseph Polsue *Lake's Parochial History, A complete parochial history of the county of Cornwall* (Truro, 1867–72).

Richard Potts (ed), *A Calendar of Cornish Glebe Terriers 1673-1735*, Devon and Cornwall Record Society, NS, vol 18 (Torquay, 1974).

M & L Quiller-Couch, *Ancient and Holy Wells of Cornwall*.

AL Rowse, *Tudor Cornwall: Portrait of a Society* (Bedford Historical Series xiv) (London, 1957).

Norman Sedding, *Norman Architecture in Cornwall* (London, 1909).

L.S. Snell, *Documents towards a History of the Reformation in Cornwall*: vol. I, *The Chantry Certificates for Cornwall* (c.1953).

T.L. Stoate (ed & publisher), *Cornwall subsidies in the reign of Henry VIII 1524 and 1543 and the benevolence of 1545* (Bristol, c1985).

J. A. Venn (comp), *Alumni Cantabrigienses.* London: Cambridge University Press, 1922-1954.

John Walker, *An ... Account of the Numbers and Sufferings of the Clergy of the Church of England ... in the late Times of the Grand Rebellion....* (London, 1713).

Appendix D: The Terrier

The terrier is the account which a church keeps of its possessions. Nowadays it is also contained in the Church Log Book of St Levan's, which is maintained by the churchwardens and of which this is a précis.

There is no longer any church hall, school, rectory or other building belonging to St Levan other than the church itself.

Church Plate:

3	Chalices, one with a lid	silver
3	pattens	2 silver, one plate
1	pyx	silver
1	ciborium	silver
1	alms dish	brass
1	tray	glass
1	wine carafe	glass
1	water carafe	glass
1	lavabo bowl	glass
1	baptismal water container	glass
1	wafer dish	silver
1	wafer box	wood
1	chandelier	
1	sanctuary lamp	silver*

*See p. 18

Notes

The references here are very brief. For full bibliographical details, see p. 119.

1. ICBS App; Bottrell (1868).
2. TNA E 179/87/7.
3. West Penwith Resources: Registers.
4. Orme (1991), p. 2.
5. Orme (1991), p. 7.
6. Brown, p. 16.
7. Olson & Padel, pp. 34-71.
8. Doble, pp. 3, 7.
9. Doble, p. 13.
10. CRO AR/2/99—membranes 1 and 2.
11. Olson & Padel, p. 42.
12. Williams, pp. 219-41.
13. There is an image of this map at Upenn.
14. Halliday, endpapers.
15. CRO WH/1/6194/1, 2: Will and probate of Jn. Harvey (1763).
16. Orme (1996), p. 97.
17. Burt, pp. 12-13; but e.g. Okasha, pp. 243-47 dates it later.
18. E.g., Henderson, pp. 304-06; also his Note in Doble, p. 13. Previous forms are in Pool, p. 40.
19. Pool, p. 37. Variants are in Place Index.
20. Foster, p. 262.
21. See Trelease for the (very weak) connexion of St Paul Aurelian with the parish and church of Paul.
22. Doble, p.10.
23. Burr, p. 8. Also Quiller-Couch, pp. 119-20.
24. Life of St Petroc, online at Celtic Christianity.
25. A full version is in Hunt; see also the lovely stained glass at St Neot's, on the edge of Bodmin Moor.
26. Borlase, p. 72.
27. West Penwith Resources: Registers.
28. Doble, pp. 7-8.
29. Howard, p 8.
30. Morris, pp. 81-4, 454.
31. See Penwith Holy Wells.
32. Crofts, p. 12.
33. See Electronic Sawyer.
34. E.g., Olson argues that it has some basis in 10th-century fact.

35. Halliday, p. 104.
36. E.g. Blair, p 18.
37. FCHR WS, p. 327. (My translation)
38. Potts, p. xi.
39. Orme (2003) online. My account of mediæval St Levan is largely based upon this work.
40. Orme (2003) online.
41. MDE, p. 6.
42. Henderson (1953), p. 55.
43. Pounds, p. 156.
44. KCC; also KCC online.
45. FCHR JG, Part I, p. 41.
46. FCHR JG, Part I, p. 43.
47. FCHR JG, Part II, p. 820.
48. Orme (2003) online.
49. FCHR JG, Part II, p. 820-21.
50. FCHR JG, Part II, p. 824-25.
51. FCHR JG, e.g. Part I, pp. 72-6, 84-7, 267.
52. Halliday, pp. 156-57.
53. Orme (2003) online.
54. Scrapbook. (I have not found his source.)
55. ODNB Moleyns.
56. Orme (2003) online.
57. Davies-Freme.
58. Duffy (2001). See Duffy (2006), p. 4 for the correct date for the start of Trychay's tenure.
59. Mattingly, p. 88 (App 1).
60. Duffy (2001), p. 84.
61. Halliday, pp. 186-87.
62. Valor Ecclesiasticus, and Snell.
63. Orme (2003) online. The calculation of St Levan's population is mine.
64. Henderson (1953), p. 55; Snell, pp 13, 15; Polsue; Orme (2003) online. Crofts, p. 50, has slightly different figures for 1536, from the Survey of First Fruits to the Crown, but the differences are minimal.
65. BU/10. Henderson (1953), p. 55.
66. Halliday, p. 199.
67. Rowse, p. 265.
68. ODNB Arundell. Also Rowse, p. 265.
69. Taylor, p. 60: "The undated Subsidy Roll [Exch Lay Subs bdle 82, no 122] of Henry VIII". This list is now published in Stoate, p 20.
70. Private communication from Prof Orme, 1 and 5 Dec 2005.
71. At least according to Hals, whose family this was.
72. Duffy (2001), pp. 130ff.

73. Duffy (2001), p. 178; Rowse, p.291.
74. Rowse, pp. 305 and 318.
75. TNA Fairchild Case: Catalogue description.
76. *Cornwall protestation returns.* Burr, p. 66 has Richard Tapper as curate, but he was the St Buryan man. Burr also shows him (and other men between 1549 and 1685) as prebendaries, which of course they were not.
77. DSB/11/1-2.
78. Walker, Part II, p. 412.
79. Halliday, pp. 240-42.
80. Coate, p. 239, quoting John Moyle, a civil war veteran.
81. Coate, pp. 239, 266 and 373.
82. Halliday, p. 262.
83. Halliday, p. 260.
84. See Hull biog, and Penney. Also Cook and Macfarlane.
85. Cook.
86. Penney, p. 12.
87. Penney, p. 16. This entry was in 1658.
88. Crofts, p. 42.
89. Coate, p. 350; Penney, p. 37.
90. Henderson, and Walker, Pt II, p. 159.
91. Polsue.
92. Burr, p. 51.
93. ODNB Ward.
94. Owen, p. 37.
95. DSB/C/196/3, 15th April 1731.
96. E.g., Buryan Book entry for the second meeting of 1747.
97. DSB/C/3.
98. DSB/C/7.
99. Harding, p. 211: referring here to a bishop's visitation.
100. DSB/C 40. Cripps, p. 88.
101. 26 George II c. 33:
102. Part VII of the Act.
103. DSB 305-415.
104. DSB/C/162.
105. DSB/C/193/8 and /9.
106. DSB/C/3.
107. DSB/C/177.
108. DSB/C/12.
109. DSB/C/17.
110. DSB/C/22. The paper is undated, but the sequence suggests it was 1715.
111. DSB/C/196/3.

112. DSB/C/127-140.
113. Harding, p. 37, quoting Rogers's *Ecclesiastical Law*.
114. Harding, pp. 35-36.
115. DSB/C/42.
116. Harding, p. 39.
117. DSB/C/31.
118. DSB/C/193/4.
119. Nankervis, pp. 5-14.
120. Transcribed in Crofts, pp. 50-52. I have not seen the original.
121. Portsmouth tithes.
122. Crofts, p. 52: "A Proposal in Relation to the Fishery" (undated).
123. Crofts, p. 54.
124. *Leges*.
125. Bowles, pp. 16-17.
126. Hosking, p. 24.
127. DSB/C/196/6.
128. Burr, p. 52.
129. DSB/C/196/1.
130. ODNB Toup.
131. St Sennen's Bells.
132. The lease was at "Lesley Aitchison's Cornwall selection," but has been sold.
133. Carew.
134. Buryan Book.
135. Hosking, p. 23: another piece by Francis (the Wit) Paynter.
136. West Penwith Resources: Registers.
137. CCEd: Jenkin; *FAE: Jenkin*.
138. Crofts, p. 43.
139. Mossman. J. Hambley Rowe (reprinted in Burr, p. 53) has him dying aged 91 in 1863. There is obviously some confusion here.
140. Bottrell, pp. 159-65; see also Hocking, pp. 10-12, 51, and Burr, p. 53.
141. "Botusfleming Incumbents."
142. Such tales are in the St Buryan church guide, and in Priestland. See also Crofts, pp. 43-44.
143. Tithe indenture.
144. mindat.org.
145. Daniel, p. 55.
146. Bishop's Licences.
147. Ecclesiastical Census.
148. Census data.
149. Daniel, p. 55.
150. Census data.
151. Tuckingmill MIs; BMD.

152. For the details of the accident, see Lardner, p. 290.
153. Kelway.
154. Kelway.
155. Census data; he is not in the 1861 census.
156. See the BL Catalogue for a list of his published works.
157. CVA.
158. PDHL:DSB.
159. BRA 833/140.
160. IGI.
161. Vestry, 13th November, 1866.
162. Tyacke.
163. Goodwin.
164. Blight, also at West Penwith Resources.
165. Vestry, 18th April, 1865.
166. Vestry, 10th July, 1866.
167. ICBS App.
168. Rectors of St Levan.
169. Vestry 1st August 1866.
170. The Sudeley Castle archivist kindly quoted me the passage.
171. Vestry, 18th April, 1865.
172. ODNB JD Sedding and ODNB E Sedding.
173. Rectors of St Levan.
174. Census data; SACC; ODNB Edalji; and Barnes.
175. *Enc Brit.*
176. Spratt.
177. Packer, p. 27.
178. QAB has 20th May.
179. DDP122/2/6/2 and /3.
180. DDP122/2/6/4.
181. DDP122/2/7/2. Letter from William H Ash, superintendent of the Telegraph Station.
182. DDP122/2/1/9.
183. Spratt: 11th April, 1880.
184. DDP122/2/1/9; also QAB.
185. Venn; census data; and *The Times.*
186. Gendall.
187. Burr, *History*, p. 42.

Bibliography

This is the key to the short references in the footnotes (see p. 114); full details are given here. Page numbers do not apply to Internet pages, although copies of printed books usually include the original page numbers. Text is, however, far more easily found by using the search facilities. (All URLs last accessed 18th October 2006 unless otherwise stated.)

Abbreviations

CRO	Cornwall Record Office
LPL	Lambeth Palace Library
PTMA	Porthcurno Telegraph Museum Archives
TNA	The National Archives
VCH	Victoria County History

Barnes: Julian Barnes, *Arthur & George* (London, 2005).
Bishop's Licences: Licences from the Bishop of Exeter, to the Dean of St. Buryan, for leave of absence on account of infirmity (19 March 1838, 15 July 1842, 16 February 1846) (CRO P23/7/1-3).
BL Catalogue: British Library Integrated Catalogue: http://catalogue.bl.uk.
Blair: John Blair, *The Church in Anglo-Saxon Society* (Oxford, 2005).
Blight: JT Blight, *Churches of West Cornwall – with notes of antiquities of the district* (London, 1865).
BMD: FreeBMD (There are other Internet sources for BMD [birth, marriage, death] data, but this is free.) http://freebmd.rootsweb.com.
Borlase: William Copeland Borlase, *The Age of the Saints, a monograph of early Christianity in Cornwall* (Truro, 1893 [1st edn 1878]).
Bottrell: William Bottrell, *Traditions and Hearthside Stories of West Cornwall* (1870, reprinted 1970).
Bottrell (1868): William Bottrell, "St Levan Church" *One and All,* July 1868.
Botusfleming Incumbents: Botus Fleming Online Parish Clerk www.cornish-ancestors.co.uk/Botusfleming/Misc%20Info/incum.htm.
Bowles: Charles Bowles, *A Short Account of the Hundred of Penwith . . .* (Shaftesbury, 1805).
Brown: H Miles Brown, *The Church in Cornwall* (Oscar Blackford: Truro, 1964).

Burge: Len Burge, *Cornish Church Sundials* (Truro, 2002).
Burr: Jeffery Burr, *A History of the Church of St Levan* (Newmill, Penzance,1994).
Burt: A Burt, A Short History and Guide Book: St Just-in-Penwith Parish Church (Church Langley, 2004).
Buryan Book: "Buryan Book of the 16th June 1744" (CRO: DSB/C/162).
Carew: "The Project Gutenberg EBook of *The Survey of Cornwall*, by Richard Carew" www.gutenberg.org/dirs/etext06/srvcr10.txt.
CCEd: Jenkin: 'Henry Jenkin (CCEd Person ID 12595)', The Clergy of the Church of England Database 1540–1835: www.theclergydatabase.org.uk(accessed 29 Apr. 2005).
Celtic Christianity: Celtic Christianity e-Library: www.lamp.ac.uk/celtic/Petroc.htm.
Census data: FreeCen: UK Census online (There are several good sources of this data, but this one is free): www.freecen.org.uk.
Coate: Mary Coate, *Cornwall in the Great Civil War and Interregnum (1642-1660)* (Truro, 1963) [1st edn 1933].
Cook: Laurence Cook, "The Exodus of the Joseph Hull Company" www.studiolarz.com/genes/bicknell/bicknell3.html.
Cooke: Ian MacNeil Cooke, *Crosses and Churchway Paths in the Land's End Peninsula West Cornwall, Vol 2: Sennen and St Levan* (Newbridge, Penzance, 2000) .
Cornwall protestation returns: *The Cornwall protestation returns 1641*; from a transcript R. M. & Glencross revised and with additional parishes transcribed by H.L. Douch, edited and published by T. L. Stoate (Bristol: 1974), p. 68. Transcribed by Rick Parsons from the facsimile on microfiche (Harry Galloway, Weston-super-Mare: 1995): http://west-penwith.org.uk/levprot.htm.
Cripps: HW Cripps, *A Practical Treatise on the Law Relating to the Church and Clergy* (3rd edition, London, 1857).
CRO AR: Manorial Records of Arundell of Lanherne and Trerice – Penwith Hundred.
CRO WH: Papers of Whitfords & Sons, and Paynter & Whitford, of St Columb Major, solicitors.
Crofts: Rev CB Crofts, *A Short History of St Buryan* (West Cornwall Field Club, Camborne, 1955).
CVA: Land Forces of Britain, the Empire and Commonwealth: Cornwall Volunteer Artillery www.regiments.org/regiments/uk/volmil-england/varty/co-av.htm.
Daniel J. Daniel, *The faith, duty, and church-membership, of a Christian. A farewell sermon,*

preached at the Land's End, Cornwall, in the parish churches of Sennen and St Levan, in the Deanery of St Buryan; June 11, 1837. To which are added, various notes and appendices, further illustrating the subjects treated in the sermon.

Davies-Freme: Rev. E. T. Davies-Freme, "A Short Description of St Uny, Lelant" (1951) http://familytreemaker.genealogy.com/users/r/o/b/Jana-K-Robertson-WA/FILE/0002page.html.

DDP: St Levan, Incumbent's papers (DDP122/2/).

DNH: Department of National Heritage, Schedule Entry Copy, National Monument No 29217: Churchyard Cross in St Levan churchyard (included 1972, affirmed 1996); and Schedule Entry Copy, National Monument No 29216: Wayside Cross in St Levan churchyard (included 1972, affirmed 1996).

Doble: The Revd GH Doble, *S Selevan: Cornish Saints Series* no 19 (a reprint in 1997 of the 3rd [1938]edition).

DSB: Papers at the CRO relating to the Deanery of St Buryan (CRO DSB).

Duffy (2001): Eamon Duffy, *The Voices of Morebath: Reformation and Rebellion in an English Village* (London, 2001).

Duffy (2006): Eamon Duffy, "Hearing Voices: on Writing the History of Reformation Morebath," (2005 Phillimore Lecture) *The Local Historian* 36: 1 (February 2006), pp. 4-16.

Ecclesiastical Census: Ecclesiastical Census for England and Wales, 1851: the Deanery of St Buryan (TNA: HO 129/311).

Electronic Sawyer: British Academy - Royal Historical Society Joint Committee on *Anglo-Saxon Charters: The Electronic Sawyer* – An online (revised, augmented, and updated) version of P. H. Sawyer, *Anglo-Saxon Charters: an Annotated List and Bibliography* (1968) www.trin.cam.ac.uk/chartwww/eSawyer.99/S%20386-458.html.

Enc Brit: Project Gutenberg EBook of the *Encyclopaedia Britannica*, (11th Edn) www.gutenberg.org/files/13600/13600-8.txt.

FAE: Jenkin: *Fasti Ecclesiae Anglicanae 1541-1857: volume 3: Canterbury, Rochester and Winchester dioceses* (1974), pp. 92-4: www.british-history.ac.uk/report.asp?compid=34626&strquery=henry%20jenkin. (Date accessed: 28 May 2006).

FCHR JG: FC Hingeston-Randolph, *The Register of John de Grandisson, Bishop of Exeter (AD 1327-1369)* (London and Exeter, 1897).

FCHR WS: FC Hingeston-Randolph, *The Register of Walter de Stapeldon [sic], Bishop of Exeter (AD 1307-1326)* (London and Exeter, 1892).

Foster: Frances Arnold Foster, *Studies in Church Dedications, or, England's Patron Saints* (London, 1899), vol ii.

Gendall: Christine Gendall, Notes on St Levan Rectory Fire, interview with Mr Ken Chiffers (unpublished private papers).

Goodwin: H Goodwin, [Reply to Tyacke], *Contemporary Review* vii, pp. 515-34.

Halliday: FE Halliday. *A History of Cornwall* (London, 2000).

Hals: William Hals, *History of Cornwall* (Truro and Exeter, parts published in 1750, some unpublished and only available now in Polsue) www.west-penwith.org.uk/gulvalh.htm.

Harding: George Harding, *A Handy Book of Ecclesiastical Law* (London, 1862).

Henderson (1953): Charles Henderson, "The Ecclesiastical History of the 109 Parishes of West Cornwall", *JRIC* n.s. 2 (1953-6).

Henderson (1962): Charles Henderson, *The Ecclesiastical History of West Cornwall* (Truro, 1962) vol ii.

Hocking: Mary Hocking, *Safari West* (St Buryan, 1996).

Hosking: Jim Hosking, *Boskenna and the Paynters* (Penzance, 1999).

Howard: FE Howard, *The Mediæval Styles of the English Parish Church: a survey of their development, design and features* (London, 1936).

Hull biography: Rev. Joseph Hull, by Sam Behling http://homepages.rootsweb.com/~sam/jhull.html.

Hunt: Robert Hunt (collected and edited by) "St Neot and the Fishes," *Popular Romances of the West of England* [1903, 3rd edition].

ICBS App: Application from the Rector of St Levan (accessed at LPL) (ICBS 6761).

IGI: Church of Jesus Christ of the Latter Day Saints: International Genealogical Index www.familysearch.org.

KCC: King's College Cambridge estates records, St Buryan deanery and the Priory of St Michael's Mount (KCAR/6/2/135/4 SBU/1 et seqq).

KCC online: King's College Cambridge: Estates Records: Cornwall www.kings.cam.ac.uk/library/archives/college/hlfproject/counties/cornwall.html.

Kelway: A. Clifton Kelway, *George Rundle Prynne: An Early Chapter in the History of the Catholic Revival* (London, 1905) transcribed at Project Canterbury http://anglicanhistory.org/bios/prynne/chapter2.html.

Langdon: Andrew Langdon, *Stone Crosses in West Penwith* (Federation of Old Cornwall Societies, 1997).

Lardner: Dionysius Lardner, *Railway economy* (London, 1850), transcribed at the

Universal Library of Carnegie Mellon University http://delta.ulib.org/ulib/data/moa/328/9ba/1fc/972/753/6/data.txt.

Leges: *"The Mediæval Sourcebook": Leges Edwardis Confessoris;* from Benjamin Thorpe, ed., *Ancient Laws and Institutes of* England, (London: Eyre & Spottiswoode, 1840), p. 442; reprinted in Roy C. Cave & Herbert H. Coulson, *A Source Book for Medieval Economic History,* (Milwaukee: The Bruce Publishing Co., 1936; reprint ed., New York: Biblo & Tannen, 1965), p. 385. www.fordham.edu/halsall/source/1115Ledwtith.html.

Lesley Aitchison's Cornwall selection: Lesley Aitchison's Cornwall selection Maps, Plans, Manuscripts, Documents, Engravings, Ephemera, etc." www.localhistory.co.uk/la/la-co.htm.

Life of St Petroc: Karen Jankulak (translator), *Vita I Petroci,* from P. Grosjean, *Analecta Bollandiana* 74 (1956), 471-96: Saint Méen Life in Paris BN Ms. lat. 9889 at Celtic Christianity (see separate entry).

Macfarlane: Sally Macfarlane, "Hopestill Holly Worden and the related Families of Holley, Allen and Hull", reprinted there with permission of author from *Wordens Past* Volume XI, No. 2, Aug. 1990 http://homepages.rootsweb.com/~worden/Holley,%20Allen%20&%20Hull.htm.

Mattingly: Joanna Mattingly, "Going A-Riding: Cornwall's Late-Mediæval Guilds Revisited" *JRIC* (2005).

MDE: George Oliver, *Monasticon Dioecesis Exoniensis* (Exeter & London, 1846).

mindat.org: mindat.org – the mineral and location database www.mindat.org/min-3211.html.

Morris: Richard Morris, *Churches in the Landscape* (London, 1997).

Mossman: Deaths column of the *West Briton,* 13th April 1838; transcribed by Julia Mossman for the Cornish-L list, 4th May 2004 http://archiver.rootsweb.com/th/read/CORNISH/2004-05/1083725929.

Nankervis: Jean Nankervis, "The St Just Easter Book and the Laudable Customs," *Treasures of the Morrab* (Penwith Local History Group, Penzance 2005).

ODNB: *Oxford Dictionary of National Biography,* Oxford University Press, 2004 www.oxforddnb.com.

ODNB Arundell: J. P. D. Cooper, 'Arundell, Humphrey (1512/13–1550)', [www.oxforddnb.com/view/article/717, accessed 25 April 2006].

ODNB E Sedding: G. C. Boase, 'Sedding, Edmund (1836–1868)', rev. Donald Findlay, [www.oxforddnb.com/view/article/25003, accessed 5 June 2006].

ODNB Edalji: Richard Davenport-Hines, 'Edalji, Shapurji (1841/2–1918)' [www.oxforddnb.com/view/article/57480, accessed 6 June 2006].

ODNB JD Sedding: Thomas Seccombe, 'Sedding, John Dando (1838–1891)', rev. Donald Findlay [www.oxforddnb.com/view/article/25004, accessed 5 June 2006].

ODNB Moleyns: Bill Smith, 'Moleyns, Adam (*d.* 1450)', [www.oxforddnb.com/view/article/18918, accessed 20 Oct 2006].

ODNB Toup: W. P. Courtney, 'Toup, Jonathan (1713–1785)', rev. M. J. Mercer [www.oxforddnb.com/view/article/27580, accessed 24th May 2006].

ODNB Ward: John Henry, 'Ward, Seth (1617–1689)', online edn, May 2006 [www.oxforddnb.com/view/article/28706, accessed 8 May 2006].

Okasha: Elizabeth Okasha, *Corpus of Early Christian Inscribed Stones of South-west Britain* (London, 1993).

Olson: Lynette Olson, *Early Monasteries in Cornwall* (Woodbridge, 1989).

Olson & Padel: Lynette Olson and OJ Padel "A Tenth-Century list of Cornish Parochial Saints", [an offprint from] *Cambridge Mediæval Celtic Studies, 12* (Winter 1986).

Orme (1991): Nicholas Orme, "From the Beginnings to 1050", in Nicholas Orme (ed) *Unity and Variety: a History of the Church in Devon and Cornwall* (Exeter, 1991)

Orme (1996): Nicholas Orme, *Church Dedications in Cornwall* (Exeter, 1996)

Orme (2003) online: "Collegiate Church of St Buryan" (draft, VCH, June, 2003) www.cornwallpast.net.

Owen: Dorothy M Owen, *Records of the Established Church in England* (British Records Association, no 1; London, 1970).

Packer: JE Packer, "Wandering Westward, an illustrated atlas" (1981, revd 1987).

PDHL:DSB: *Parliamentary Debates* (House of Lords), 3rd Series, 27th May 1850 (Vol. 111, cols 366-368).

Penney: Norman Penney (transcribed and edited by), *Record of the sufferings of Quakers in Cornwall 1655-1686* (Friends Historical Society, London: 1928).

Penwith Holy Wells: Laurence Hunt, The Holy Wells of West Penwith, Cornwall http://people.bath.ac.uk/liskmj/living-spring/sourcearchive/fs3/fs3lh1.htm.

Place Index: An Index to the Historical Place Names of Cornwall http://cornovia.org.uk/ihpnc/a_b.html.

Polsue: Joseph Polsue *Lake's Parochial History, A complete parochial history of the county of Cornwall* (Truro, 1867–72) http://west-penwith.org.uk/burian2.htm#clergy (and elsewhere at this site).

Pool: PAS Pool, *Place-Names of West Penwith* (1985).
Portsmouth tithes: University of Portsmouth, "The Tithe Survey of England and Wales—Tithes" http://tiger.iso.port.ac.uk:7785/www/web.html?p=tithes.
Potts: Richard Potts (ed), *A Calendar of Cornish Glebe Terriers 1673-1735*, Devon and Cornwall Record Society, NS, vol 18 (Torquay, 1974).
Pounds: NJG Pounds, "Taxation and Wealth in Late Mediæval Cornwall", *JRIC*, n.s. 6 (1971).
Preston-Jones: Ann Preston-Jones, *St Levan's Well: Archaeological conservation work* (Cornwall Archaeological Unit, March 2001).
Priestland: Gerald Priestland, *PS, with Love to Cornwall* (New Mill, 1992).
QAB: Queen Anne's Bounty records: St Levan Church (accessed at LPL) (E2912).
Quiller-Couch: M & L Quiller-Couch, *Ancient and Holy Wells of Cornwall*.
Rectors of St Levan: Revd LA Tonkin, "An Account of the Rectors of St Levan" (1934), in the Scrapbook (see separate entry) (CRO P122/2/31/22).
Rowse: AL Rowse, *Tudor Cornwall: Portrait of a Society* (Bedford Historical Series xiv) (London, 1957).
SACC: Archive catalogue of St Augustine College, Canterbury at Canterbury Cathedral Archives (CCA-U88/A/2/7/C/21A) www.canterbury-cathedral.org/archives.html.
Scrapbook: Scrapbook collected by the Revd Charles Abdy in 1959-60 (CRO: P122/2/31).
Sedding: Norman Sedding, *Norman Architecture in Cornwall* (London, 1909).
Snell: L.S. Snell, *Documents towards a History of the Reformation in Cornwall*: vol. I, *The Chantry Certificates for Cornwall* (c.1953).
Spratt: Diary of Mr George Spratt 1871–1885, Cable & Wireless Archive Eastern Telegraph Co Ltd) (PTMA: DOC/ETC/5/70/).
St Sennen's Bells: "St Sennen's Bells" from Dunkin, *The Church Bells of Cornwall* (1878). www.communigate.co.uk/twc/stsennenchurchbellringers/page3.html.
Stoate: T.L. Stoate (ed & publisher), *Cornwall subsidies in the reign of Henry VIII 1524 and 1543 and the benevolence of 1545* (Bristol, c1985).
Taylor: Canon Thomas Taylor, proof copy of an unpublished volume of the VCH at the Courtney Library, Truro (c 1908) (VCH: Cornwall Topography).
Thomas (I): Charles Thomas, *And Shall These Mute Stones Speak? Post-Roman Inscriptions in Western Britain* (Cardiff, 1994).

Thomas (2): Charles Thomas, report of his work in the chancel of St Levan church in 1997 (unpublished MS).
The Times: *The Times* Digital Archive.
Tithe indenture: Tithe indenture: 25th December 1820, endorsed 25th May 1841 (CRO: BRA 833/140).
TNA E 179: Records of the Exchequer: King's Remembrancer: Particulars of Account and other records relating to Lay and Clerical Taxation.
TNA Fairchild Case: Exchequer: King's Remembrancer: Barons' Depositions (TNA, 39 Eliz. Trin. E133/8/1319).
Trelease: G. M. Trelease, *A History of Paul Church* (2006).
Tuckingmill MIs: Tuckingmill Monumental Inscriptions http://freepages.genealogy.rootsweb.com/~camborneopc/surnamestuckingmillA-C.htm.
Tyacke: Joseph Sidney Tyacke, "The Congé d'Élire": a paper read at the Autumn Session of the Ruridecanal Synod of Penwith, Cornwall (London, 1867)
Upenn: University of Pennsylvania English department http://www.english.upenn.edu/~bushnell/english-30/gallery.html.
Valor Ecclesiasticus: J. Caley (ed) *Valor Ecclesiasticus tempore Henrici VIII auctoritate regia institutus*, 6 vols (London, Record Commission, 1810-24).
Venn: Cambridge University Alumni, 1261-1900 Records, a digitalised version searchable at http://ancestry.com of J. A. Venn (comp), *Alumni Cantabrigienses.* (London: Cambridge University Press, 1922-1954).
Vestry: St Levan Parish Vestry Minutes (CRO: DDP122/8/1).
Walker: John Walker, *An Attempt towards Recovering an Account of the Numbers and Sufferings of the Clergy of the Church of England, heads of Colleges, Fellows, Scholars, &c, who were sequester'd, harrass'd [sic], &c in the late Times of the Grand Rebellion....* (London, 1713).
West-Penwith Resources: West Penwith Resources http://west-penwith.org.uk/Levan.htm.
West Penwith Resources – Registers: West Penwith Resources http://west-penwith.org.uk/Levan.htm and click through to St Levan parish, and then the relevant registers.
Williams: NJA Williams, " 'Saint' in Cornish" *Cornish Studies* NS 7.

List of Subscribers

The Parish Priest, the Revd Brin Berriman and the St Levan Parochial Church Council wish to acknowledge the considerable financial support received from the Friends of St Levan Church, a bequest from the estate of Sir George Sinclair, and individual donations from the subscribers whose names are listed below. Without their generosity, the publication of this Guide and History of St Levan Parish Church would not have been possible.

Ted & Barbara Atter
Sir John & Lady Banham
The Revd Brin & Mrs Cheryl Berriman
Drs Melissa Hardie & Philip Budden
Lt Col & Mrs Lawrence Burr
Mrs Jeffery Burr
Dr & Mrs WG Burton
Janis & Fred Byott
The Revd. & Mrs FH Chalk
Valery Cons
Sally Corbet
Trish & Adrian Cox
Phil & Edith Crow
Mrs C Cullen
Gillian Earl
Mr & Mrs Bob Ellis
Mr Christopher Evans
The Friends of St Levan
Mrs Mary Faure
Diane L Fowlkes
Mrs Rose Ginn
Mr Bobbie George
Peter & Anita George
Dr James Goldie *in memoriam*
Mrs Pamela Goldie
Mrs WA Goodwin
Ann Grace

Jonathan & Elizabeth Groves
Mrs G A Hart
Demelza & Renny Henderson
Mr Trevor & Mrs Gill Hogben
Fiona Holdaway
Daphne B Holland
Bolitho Hosking
Alan Hoyle
Carenza Hugh-Jones
David & Bridget Hugh-Jones
John & Jackie Iles
David & Sue James
Michael & Jean Jeffries
Martin & Kate Jennings
Lynn & Bob Kirkup
Jeremy Knight
Mark Lanyon
The Revd. Dr Richard Legg
Mr & Mrs H D Malyan
Mr & Mrs Dennis Mundy
John Nash
Joyce Peters
The Revd. Helen & Mr Robert Poole
The Porthcurno Telegraph Museum
Ros & Burt Prigg
David & Patricia Rayfield
Dorothy & Alan Reed Legacy

Betty Rickarby Bell
Robin Rickarby
Jimmy & Carolyn Scobie
Jonathan & Sally Scott
Charles & Nicky Sinclair
Sir George Sinclair's Legacy
Lady Sinclair
James & Mary St Aubyn
St Buryan Garage Ltd

Mr Richard Sweet & Mr Alan Singer
Mr & Mrs John & Lucy Taylor
Frank & Bobbie Thomas
Morgan Walton
Alan & Susan Wear
Wendy & Doug White
Chris & Pat Wiblin
Judy Woodman
Jane & Geoff Wright

Memorial to Evelyn Bennett, teacher *(pew-end 1):*
Many people remember one teacher with especial fondness. Sir George Sinclair (1912-2005) remembered Evelyn Trimer Bennett. Before he was sent away to boarding school, he went to the village school in Porthcurno (the building just below the Post Office), where he was taught by Miss Bennett, the Rector's daughter. Some years later he dedicated a beautifully carved pew-end to her; above is the dedication carved inside the pew. Sir George's recent legacy to St Levan has helped fund the publication of this book, and this reminder of the gratitude due to him and all other subscribers seems a fitting note on which to end.

Acknowledgements

The following people helped me in researching and writing this Guide and History, and there is space here merely to list them. I hope that they will accept this scant mention as an earnest of my heartfelt thanks:

Jeffery Burr (the late author of the 1994 *History of St Levan Church*, whom I never met), the Church of England Record Centre, the Cornwall Record Office, the London Library (and in particular its country-members service), the Cornish Studies Library, the Courtney Library, the Devon Record Office, the Family Records Centre, Christine Gendall, Jim Hosking, Bridget Hugh-Jones, Jeremy Knight, Lambeth Palace Library, Joanna Mattingly, numerous members of the e-lists Mediev-L, mediaeval-religion, anglicanhistory, H-Albion and VICTORIA, the Morrab Library, Jean Nankervis, Nicholas Orme, Oliver Padel, Rick Parsons, Robert Poole, Porthcurno Telegraph Museum and Archive, Leslie Sparrow, Lucy and John Taylor, The National Archives, Alison Weeks, and Christopher Wiblin.

The Internet has been indispensable in researching this book: I mention only the Canterbury Project, Church Plans Online, the Clergy of the Church of England Database, Project Gutenberg, the ODNB Online, The Times Online, and the VCH.

At the start, Joanna Mattingly gave me a private tutorial on St Levan and the study of Cornish churches; later, Nicholas Orme read part of an early draft of the History and made many helpful comments; and similarly, Christopher Wiblin commented on an early draft of the Guide. Donna Anton has been an excellent layout editor, patient, alert and wise. Despite all this expert help, support and advice, there will still be errors. Responsibility for them is clearly mine.

Susan Hoyle
Alsia Mill
October 2006

About the Author

Susan Hoyle graduated from Somerville College Oxford with a degree in Philosophy, Politics and Economics, although her passion has always been for history. After a varied career, including the civil service, the Open University, and running a public-transport pressure-group, she joined British Rail, first as a PR officer and then as Director of Quality Through People. She has also been a freelance writer. After British Rail was privatised, she and her husband travelled around Britain on a narrow boat for 18 months, during which time she was able to visit many parish churches.

Susan has had several articles published. Recently she wrote the section on St Levan Church for *The Book of St Levan*, which started her interest in this lovely church and in the Deanery of St Buryan. She is currently working on a short life of the last Dean of St Buryan, the Hon and Very Revd Fitzroy Henry Richard Stanhope (1787-1864).

She lives in St Buryan parish with her husband and some hens. Their children are all grown and gone.